P9-CKR-561

NC
999.4
.H 64
A 4
Holmes
Designing pictorial symbols

DATE DUE

Laramie County Community College
Instructional Resources Center
Cheyenne, Wyoming 82001

2-28-86 P030427 B+T

DESIGNING PICTORIAL SYMBOLS

By Nigel Holmes

with Rose DeNeve

LCCC LIBRARY

WATSON-GUPTILL PUBLICATIONS/NEW YORK

To Laurie and Rowland

Copyright © 1985 by Watson-Guptill Publications
First published 1985 in New York by Watson-Guptill Publications,
a division of Billboard Publications, Inc.,
1515 Broadway, New York, N.Y. 10036

Library of Congress Cataloging in Publication Data

Holmes, Nigel, 1942–
   Designing pictorial symbols.

   Bibliography: p.
   Includes index.
   1. Holmes, Nigel, 1942–   2. Signs and symbols—
Psychological aspects.   3. Graphic arts—Technique.
I. DeNeve, Rose.   II. Title.
NC999.4.H64A4   1985   741.6   85-3143
ISBN 0-8230-1327-8

Distributed in the United Kingdom by Phaidon Press Ltd., Littlegate
House, St. Ebbe's St., Oxford

All rights reserved. No part of this publication may be
reproduced or used in any form or by any means—graphic,
electronic, or mechanical, including photocopying, recording,
taping, or information storage and retrieval systems—without
written permission of the publisher.

Manufactured in U.S.A.

First Printing, 1985
1 2 3 4 5 6 7 8 9 10 / 90 89 88 87 86 85

ACKNOWLEDGMENTS

IN ENGLAND in the 1930s, a designer, sadly now "unknown," drew a series of pictorial logos for the Spratts pet-food company, with each logo made up of the letters in the name Spratts. There was a cat, a bird, and a dog; but by far the most used version was the dog. It endured as a trademark for a long time and was certainly the first bit of graphic design that made any impression on me, coming into our home as it did on the cans of dog food we fed to our pet dachshund. That Spratts logo was the start of something small in my life—usually about half an inch square, in fact.

Now, my thanks go to Stephen Kliment, who has shepherded this book through with a kind and understanding touch, beginning with his wonderful suggestion that Rose DeNeve should do a lot of the writing. Rose spent many hours interviewing me for the chapters on *Time* symbols, American Renewal, and the *Radio Times* work, then went away to write it all down and deliver her typescript exactly on time. (Others at Watson-Guptill need acknowledgment of their patience in waiting for the rest of the book!) It was a great pleasure to collaborate with a real professional.

Barbara Klinger was an extremely precise and helpful editor; Candace Raney coordinated all the little bits and pieces; and Bob Fillie produced a design which held them all together with an elegant glue.

In England, I would like to thank Charlie Riddell, who as art director of New Society in the late sixties gave me such short deadlines for illustrations that I had to develop a clear "symbolic" style to meet them. My thanks also to David Driver, for whom I did about two hundred black-and-white symbols at the British Broadcasting Corporation's *Radio Times* before coming to America.

To all my colleagues at *Time* (who refer to the symbols as "dingles"), I thank you for help and advice. Especially I should mention Jack Geist, who takes great pains to ensure that the dingles line up with the text properly, and Jay Dowd, who makes sure that the tiny things are not lost amongst the hundreds of other images that he is sending off to be processed in a *Time* week. As ever, I am grateful to Nino Telak for his assistance—in this particular instance, for his invaluable mechanical help with the cover, and the redrawing of many of the *Radio Times* pieces.

My wife Laurie has put up with a second book in our lives with quite remarkable calm. More than that, she has researched from New York to the Wiltshire Downs and has still managed to perform the role that has long been referred to in our home as "the ideas department." Many thanks and ♥.

Contents

CHAPTER THREE

American Renewal: Story of a Print Campaign   **102**

Step-by-step through all the stages in the development of one symbol for a project urging America to revitalize itself in every facet of politics, business, and life.

CHAPTER FOUR

Sports Symbols: *The Radio Times* 112

Ten years of sporting signage from the pages of a British consumer weekly magazine, from horse racing to table tennis, with 14 sports in between.

CHAPTER FIVE

A Gallery of Symbols 130

A personal collection of examples from around the world, introduced by a discussion of the signage from seven Olympic games starting with London in 1984.

CHAPTER ONE
An Introduction to Pictorial Symbols

Fifty thousand years ago, man made his mark—simple abstract strokes cut into rock or bone. They were his lists of animals seen or caught and his notes of the passage of time—early calendars. Over thousands of years, the marks developed into picture-symbols of the animals and other objects that he felt he needed to record and leave for others to see. By 4,000 B.C. the Sumerians were using two thousand pictographs in their clay-tablet writing. Two thousand years later, the Egyptians were making do with just twenty-four signs, and man had begun to replace picture writing with phonetic writing. Symbols no longer stood for concrete objects but for words and sounds, and languages evolved as abstract systems describing anything that had or has to be communicated. With one hundred languages and five thousand dialects in use today, communication is perhaps more complex than ever.

Nearly three hundred years ago, the German philosopher and mathematician Baron Gottfried Wilhelm Von Leibnitz imagined that someday there would exist a universal system of pictorial symbols that could be read in all languages without having to be translated. Since then, many efforts have been made to produce written communications that are internationally understood; Esperanto, for example, is an artificial language invented in 1887. It is supposed to be easily learned by most people familiar with European language-types. Semantography, invented in 1949 by the Australian Charles Bliss, is an honest attempt to create a pictorial "alphabet." The hundred semi-abstract images in Bliss's system were designed to be used on an interchangeable typewriter "golf ball," but they still needed to be learned. Nearer the subject of this book are Otto Neurath's pictorial symbols. With his ISOTYPE* he does not try to supply a complete visual equivalent of a language that can encompass all human emotions, nuances of feeling, and layers of meaning (as Bliss claimed for his system). Neurath (1882-1945) did, however, produce symbols that could be understood by anyone.

The ISOTYPE symbols were drawn by a team of artists under Neurath's direction at the Gesellsschafts-und-Wirtschaftsmuseum (Social and Economic Museum) in Vienna. The leading artists were Gert Arntz and Augustin Tschinkel. Beginning as "little drawings" in 1925, the symbols went through a period of stylization in 1926-27, during which time Neurath insisted that the artists cut the

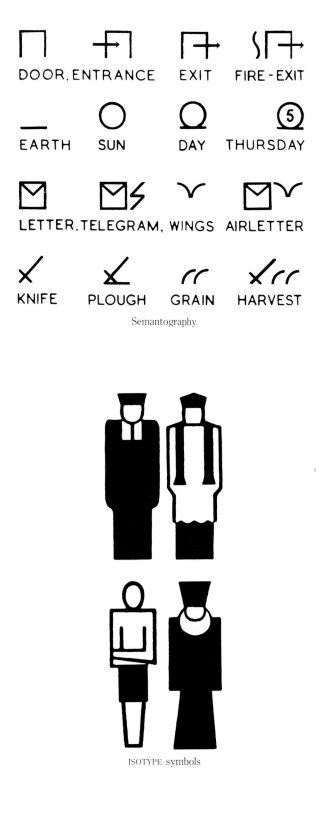

Semantography

ISOTYPE symbols

*International System Of Typographic Picture Education

shapes from paper, or use lino cuts, to train them to simplicity. By 1930, the team had refined the idea of the pictorial symbol.

Neurath firmly believed that pictures are a better method of receiving new information and knowledge than words alone; thus he returned to an earlier system of communication, one based on pure sign-messages, such as the pictures men had painted on the cave walls of Lascaux in France and Altamira in northern Spain, or the petroglyphs that American Indians had scratched and pecked into the rocks of the southwestern United States.

Today, as we travel more but are increasingly lazy about learning other people's languages, the role of the sign has become an important one. At airports, on roads, and in hotels, the pictorial symbol gets its message across quickly, whether we are driving past it at 50 mph in America or standing still in Japan or India.

The evidence of this greater use and reliance on symbols is all around us. As you speed by that road sign showing falling rocks, you may glance down to the dashboard and be reminded by a tiny, flashing oil can that it is time to top up. Advertisements for real-estate companies use miniature drawings to describe the particulars of a property on offer; hotels outline their services with symbols for the swimming pool, TV in every room, no dogs allowed, room with bath, and so on. Your washing machine is loaded with symbolic representations of the correct water-temperature, spinning action, or amount of detergent to be put in. And as you put a new roll of film into a camera which itself has pictures engraved into it, you need only to look at the illustrations on the box to be able to set the right exposure.

We are told that the first glimmer of two-way communication between a child and its parents is a response to a smile. Show an infant a piece of paper with nothing on it but a line that curves upwards at the ends, and the infant will smile back. There is something about the shape that not only looks like a mouth in a smiling position, but also contains the essence of the emotion involved. As the child grows up, the recognition of that particular symbol may become dulled by its repeated use—the familiar yellow button has taken the edge off a primal response and turned it into a visual cliché that ranks along with the "Mona Lisa" and Grant Wood's "American Gothic" as the rip-off images most to be avoided in any graphic-designer's vocabulary.

This book will not deal with trademarks, however pictorial (like Mr. Peanut); company logos; or abstract signs. Rather it will discuss pictorial symbols which tell a story, teach you how to do something, or simply indicate a fact, as "here are the gymnastics." These symbols are usually recognized by their context. In the milieu of the Olympic

games, a particular sign means yachting; away from that context, it could be very hard to make out what the figure is supposed to be doing. Similarly, an English road-construction sign, when seen in its proper setting, is a picture of a man digging his shovel into a pile of earth. Out of that situation, it is just as obviously a man struggling to get his umbrella open!

Context, then, is important. Each of the symbols shown in the next chapter, for example, was developed to link a particular group of complex stories appearing in *Time* magazine; as such, each symbol was surrounded by words and was reinforced by the reader's knowledge of the subject under discussion. While the symbols can stand alone, they were not actually designed to do so. They are part of the editorial content of the magazine and will always be seen in that context.

THE SYMBOL AND ITS ELEMENTS

A symbol stands for something. It is visually precise; it attempts to get at the essence of an idea—either by being a literal, miniature drawing, or by being a non-literal, visual metaphor. A symbol can give an identity to a subject and, by repeated use, can come to equal it.

The elements a designer uses to create a quickly understood symbol are the basic graphic shapes: circles, square, diamonds, and so forth. Each comes with its own meanings, and when put together with each other in different configurations, the shapes can become very potent. Consider the circle: the single zero sign is a ball, a hole, a disc, a wheel, or nothing; it can be any or all of these things before another mark is used with it. The circle may be purposefully ambiguous, but if the context rules out ambiguity, the addition of the minutest detail will transform the circle into a host of ideas that are not ambiguous. On the right, from the top down, the circle has become a face, sphere, mouth, tennis ball, baby, globe, doughnut, wheel, apple, Saturn, last-quarter moon, pill, clock, piechart, sun, eye, 12 o'clock, 3 o'clock, 6 o'clock. Add color, and the range of possibilities widens further: red for *stop*, green for *go*.

But a reliance on color can be dangerous, too. A red star means Russia. In other colors or in black, it would not have the same meaning. As a designer, you must be sure that red is technically possible for the reproduction of your design. Without the red, the star returns to its other meanings—stardom, first class, outstanding achievement, Hollywood, etc.; or worse, the symbol could be confused with other nations: China's yellow star on a red background for instance, or the United States' white on blue.

In the same way, complex tonal variations in the design of a symbol are generally not workable. The

use of the art at a small scale is, more often than not, part of the design brief, and tones will not stand up to the sort of reduction necessary. Besides, the reduction of an idea to its simplest elements rules out gray areas in thinking in much the same way that it works against the grays in between the designer's black and white.

Not that all symbols are small. In Britain's Iron Age, huge figures were cut into the side of the chalk hills of southern England, and many survive today. The earth, only a foot or two deep, was dug away to reveal the white chalk underneath. Although the exact purpose of the figures is debated, the 360-foot-long white horse at Uffington, the "long man" of Wilmington, and the Cerne Abbas Giant were either religiously or militarily symbolic, and they were presumably large so as to be seen from a great distance. They were also simple in design. Perhaps they were the road signs that guided early man.

PITFALLS

In the nineteenth century, trademarks were little pictures. In the early twentieth century, the Shell Oil symbol started out as a drawing of a real shell; it then went through a number of changes before arriving at the simpler graphic arrangement of lines in use today. The name Shell, incidentally, was adopted as a result of the seashells originally carried by the company's trade ships returning from the East. Although shell cargoes were eventually replaced by oil, the original name stuck. Few people know of this association between oil and shell, and there is no reason why they should; the symbol is an example of meaning through association and repetition, rather than a direct symbol of the subject matter. But sometimes a sign is misunderstood and is obviously a failure. This may happen by an inexact simplification of a graphic shape. When reduced to their basic forms, for example, certain kinds of trees could easily be confused with an atomic explosion. Thus a symbol such as the one shown here could have two very different meanings.

One of the most universally understood symbols is the arrow; this is both an advantage and a disadvantage, because the arrow means too many things. Almost any subject can use an arrow in some form as a symbol: it denotes speed, forward, upward, down, across, the future, history, reaching out, shuttling back and forth, attack, a rise or fall in the economy, push, here, you. Look through books of trademarks and symbols and see how often the arrow has been used. Only in conjunction with another design element does it become fully potent—really representing something other than the general notions listed above. By being so universal, it has come to mean very little.

1900

1904

1909

1930

1948

1955

1961

1971

The idea that a sign easily understood in one country will mean the same thing in another country is a common pitfall. The straw boater has nothing to do with political activity in England. There, it is a perfect vehicle for putting across ideas about the upper classes and their summer sports—rowing in particular. In America, the boater tossed up into the air is all that is needed for a political convention. U.S. elections also have a symbol that is unknown elsewhere—the voting lever. Because this "symbol" is actually a drawing of a piece of machinery found in some American voting booths, it should not follow that such a narrowly focused idea will stand for the whole process of an election. It is rather like assuming that the very particular shape of an English electrical plug could be a worldwide symbol for electricity. The plug looks quite different from an American one, or for that matter a French one, and would create confusion rather than transmit an efficient message.

Designers need not always think that their work is going to be internationally visible; if their work is going to be seen only in the United States, for instance, the voting lever may be a perfectly good image for the intended audience. However, the ballot box (perhaps with a simplified hand inserting a piece of paper into it) is also very much about elections, and it has the advantage of being more readily understood by a larger audience. To use an "old-fashioned" image such as this is sometimes the best answer. There may be only a few places in

the States where this kind of voting procedure is still used, but as a symbol, the ballot box has never ceased to be the most instantly recognized mark of an election. As another example, try drawing the most up-to-date telephone, to represent that form of communication; it is too smoothed-out to mean anything. The slightly outdated handset still does the trick, although I'll allow that it is just about acceptable now to put buttons instead of a dial on the front!

Finally, let no one think that the stylized figures that appear in pictographs are cold and devoid of human characteristics and emotion. Look at this figure of a worker. He is unemployed. Not only is there no doubt about that, but the man's very sadness comes through the simple drawing. He is shivering. He is looking back, rather than to the future. So much can be conveyed by so few shapes.

Figures such as this can too easily be dismissed as "stick-men," "pin-men," or "robot people," but in fact, they evoke a whole host of emotions that belie their simple execution. And that perhaps is the point: to evoke rather than describe. The mere slope of the shoulders (as in this example) or the thrust of a pair of jauntily marching legs can convey a range of feelings, from pity to optimism. Those feelings are inside us already. One doesn't need a photograph to touch the right chord and bring them out.

Keep the symbol simple, but let the feelings run wild!

CHAPTER TWO

Time Pieces

SYMBOLS ARE such small things; it is easy to give them little regard. It was only after I'd done a few for *Time* that I decided to keep them together in a file; I was surprised at how many there had actually been. It seemed, whether I liked it or not, that I was going to end up with another collection of tearsheets containing minute examples of my work, much as I had first done in England.

Well, I did like it, and I was well trained when Walter Bernard redesigned *Time* in 1977 and needed, on occasion, a device to link more than one story on a given subject. The idea of doing a pictorial symbol for this purpose appealed to me; it was not to be used decoratively (that is, just to dress up a page, as an art director's whim) but it had a real job to do, which was to let the reader see that a story had companion pieces related to it. For instance, in our coverage of the chemical-plant disaster in India in 1984, there were six related articles. These included the news report, a think-piece about the terrible event, and four additional features: living next to similar plants around the world, the industry's own efforts in keeping the job safe, the question about whether it could happen in the U.S., and finally a look at the financial and business implications for the company concerned.

The symbol was used six times, at the start of each new topic, but some of the articles were separated from a preceding one by advertisements. In all, the articles covered twenty-five pages, of which eleven were ads.

Some may argue that all the articles could have been strung together with less stopping and starting. By breaking the total story into sections, however, *Time* does two things. Firstly, it allows the reader to get a great deal of information in manageable chunks (it is after all a magazine—and the dentist may well get through his first appointment sooner than you'd thought!), and secondly, it allows the editor to assign different writers to different parts of the story, thus making complete coverage more manageable when there may be very little time in which to produce it.

In 1977, I was more often than not drawing the symbols in black with the use of one other color, probably red. Although now there is four-color availability on every page, I sometimes long for the simplicity of the days when the limited means at one's disposal eliminated unnecessary "decorative" thinking and focused the mind on the essence of the subject at hand. As technology marches on, we should beware of embracing it purely for the sake of keeping up, and if two colors are the most direct way of communicating, then two colors should be used, and technology can show off in other areas.

MAN OF THE YEAR

December 19, 1977; December 17, 1979; January 3, 1983

SINCE 1928, when Charles Lindbergh was named *Time*'s first Man of the Year, the magazine's editors have selected annually one personality who has figured prominently in the news or who has somehow altered the course of human events. Although the final selection is made by the editor-in-chief and the managing editor from suggestions submitted by senior editors and correspondents, *Time* readers also send in hundreds of their own nominations.

In 1977 and 1979, it was decided to note the readers' suggestions in the weekly letters-to-the-editor column, which generally discusses topics that appeared two weeks previously. Hence, the picture on the small *Time* cover that usually appears on the letters page was to be replaced by a symbol indicating the topic, "Who will be the next Man of the Year?"

The symbol that appeared in 1977 was one of the first designs I did for *Time*. Since the winner's portrait always appeared on the cover of the magazine, the real visual question was, "Whose face will it be?" I made two small, tentative sketches in my notebook (1)—the first using a question mark as the "i" in the *Time* logo, the other using the logo as the dot under the question mark.

In looking at this second idea, I considered the negative space inside the question mark: its roundness suggested a face upon which features could be hung. I executed two versions of this idea, each with the question mark dropped out from inside a black circle (2–3). For the final art, I chose the sketch where the question mark breaks through the outer circle (3). I felt it made the symbol more active and made the circle itself a graphic element by breaking it up into two dissimilar black shapes.

In 1979, I designed a second Man-of-the-Year symbol, one that visually turned the first symbol inside out. Although my first sketches (4) included a face with a question mark inside and a "digitized" face (perhaps for a modern man?), the curving surface of the question mark proved irresistible. This time, the facial features were hung on the outside of the mark, and after a few trials to calculate their positions and shapes ·(5), I statted up the sketches and filled them in with black marker (6). From this I did a tracing of the most pleasing (7) and went to finished art (8).

A third instance calling for a Man of the Year symbol was not in anticipation of the naming, but as a result of it: the "man" selected to represent 1982 was not a man at all, nor even a person, but the personal computer; it was the only time, I might add, such an unhuman selection has been made. Hence, for the first time, *Time* needed a symbol for a Machine of the Year. The symbol was to tie together various elements of the cover story.

The crux of the solution was that this story wasn't just about a computer, nor the world of computers, but about the computer and you and me—a machine that, it was imagined, would soon be in every home.

The symbol attempts to convey this idea quite literally by combining a computer keyboard and screen with the roof of a house and was conceived to work in both black-and-white and color (9). The design needed little development before it was cleaned up for the final art (10–11).

At the last minute, a decision was made not to use the symbol after all. There were so many different strands to the story, and the symbol was to appear so many times, that the editors feared it would become too intrusive. A special heading that read "Machine of the Year" was designed by Michael Doret to take its place as a linking element.

Whatever the editorial reasons for not using it, this symbol was nonetheless successful in its own terms. It was comprised of two easily recognizable elements already part of people's visual vocabularies. In short, it was a neat solution, and although I understood the logic of its rejection, I was sorry to see it go.

5

6

7   8

9

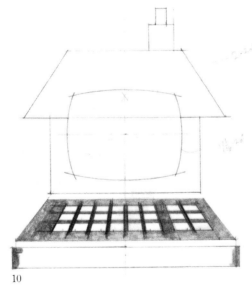

10

11

ENERGY
THE SEVEN LEAN YEARS
December 22, 1980

THE PRICE of oil had been rising dramatically for some time, but especially during 1979 and 1980, and *Time* ran a series of stories looking at alternative sources of energy. President Reagan had just been elected, and Americans were already beginning to use less energy.

My first idea for a symbol was an "energetic" one—a vibrating lightning bolt (1). But this image also symbolizes "electricity," which is after all a type of energy, not a source.

So the symbol became more generalized and at the same time more complex. Since the sources of energy being discussed included oil, nuclear power, coal, water, and the sun, I fitted images for each of these into one compact shape (2). From this marker sketch, I made a tracing (3) on which to base the final two-color art (4).

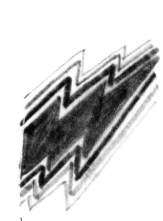

1

2

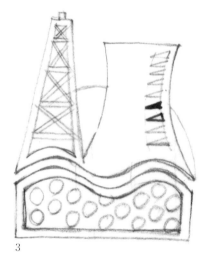

3

4

THE HUMBLING OF OPEC
February 7, 1983

IT WAS A TIME of gross infighting among the thirteen members of the Organization of Petroleum Exporting Countries (OPEC), and meetings of their delegates in Geneva to discuss the worldwide oil glut that was forcing prices down had ended in complete failure. There was even some question as to whether OPEC itself would survive.

My first sketches tried to visualize an OPEC in trouble. Although no one in the U.S. would shed a tear at the break-up of the so-called cartel, OPEC members certainly would, and this thought was the basis of these early sketches (1).

Here, I tried to utilize the OPEC initials as the features of a crying face. It was necessary that the face not look particularly Arab, for OPEC includes some non-Arab states as well. At this point, I also sketched a crying eye within a barrel-like shape, but felt this image was too ambiguous.

I proceeded to develop the OPEC face (2). I felt the "C" in the acronym was particularly expressive as a mouth in pain, and it was a matter of finding similarly suitable forms for the other letters. But by the time I had made my sixth attempt (3), I saw that the face idea wasn't working, and I went on to something else.

This new direction was more straightforward. A quick sketch of an oil derrick as the obvious OPEC symbol (4) led to the solution of a derrick drowning in its own oil (5). The metaphor was appropriate: the allied states were producing so much crude that their organization—and its prices—could no longer stay afloat.

In tracing this sketch for the final art, I feel the figure lost some of its vitality (6), much of which came from the roughly drawn lines of the sketch. I also feel the solution would have been more successful if the derrick had occupied a larger part of the circle.

The final was printed in three colors: blue for the sky and black for the oily sea, with the derrick in red for drama.

NUCLEAR ENERGY: Bombing Out?
February 13, 1984

 THIS SYMBOL was designed for a report on the nuclear industry, which wasn't doing as well as had been anticipated. Thus, the solution had to connote a negative feeling as well as the idea of nuclear power.

The American public already had a powerful symbol for nuclear power in its visual vocabulary—a cooling tower—and I drew two basic versions of this familiar form. The first of these (1) included a vapor cloud, which I visualized rising and floating up behind the headline type. But vapor, which is white or colorless, couldn't easily be conveyed. I would either have to draw it as a gray cloud or use a second color, such as red. But either of these solutions would change the meaning of the symbol.

The second variation relied on the tower alone as a symbol (2), and in developing it for the final art, it became a matter of selecting the right colors and refining the shape. The tower walls, for example, were not arcs from a circle, but curved lines yielding a figure broader at its base than its top (3).

In the final solution (4), the tower stands alone against a blue sky, its bright red color being the only indication of an industry in trouble.

POLAND'S ORDEAL
December 23, 1981

IT WAS A BAD time for Poland. The Solidarity strike, started in 1980 in Gdansk, had met strong reprisals: Lech Walesa had been arrested (and was on his way to being named *Time* Man of the Year); Russia had marched into Poland to squelch all opposition, placing the nation under martial law. The best symbol for *Time*'s report on these developments was one that would convey the idea of Russia crushing the Poles.

My first idea was sketched in two versions of a red fist set within a descending black arrow (1), but this did not seem powerful enough. Nor did it adequately represent the parties involved. A second attempt, a red hammer and sickle marching in Cossack boots (2), was no more satisfactory—it was a bit too cute. But the Cossack boot seemed a viable element, and it inspired the ultimate symbol (3).

Because the red-and-white Polish flag was fresh in people's minds at the time, and because the colors were also associated with the Solidarity movement, which had received broad American support, the Polish flag was the correct image to be placed beneath the heel of the boot. While the final symbol (4) might not have worked earlier or later in the situation, it was right for the time because of current visual vocabulary.

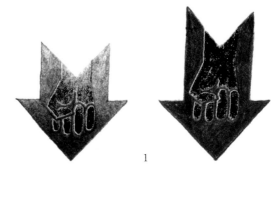

1

2

3

4

GREEK ELECTIONS
November 2, 1981

OCCASIONALLY an event that receives only summary coverage in the domestic editions of *Time* is expanded for international readers. Such was the case with coverage of elections held in Greece near the close of 1981.

Like many *Time* symbols, this one was developed at the last minute, after all the stories on the subject had come in, and because of the situation's complexity, it had to convey both "Greece" and "problems."

Working from the premise of Greek architecture being an obvious symbol for Greece, I gathered some references (1) and did a cropped drawing of the top of an Ionic column (2). This said "Greece" all right, but it didn't say "problems." Other ideas—a vote being cast into a Grecian urn (3) and some architectural solutions (4–5)—were similarly unsatisfactory. Hearing of my difficulties, a *Time* editor suggested an image of the Parthenon collapsing, but this would not be the easiest symbol to draw.

By Friday night's closing, I still hadn't a symbol, and time was running out. I decided to go with the editor's idea, and I developed a drawing of a classical Greek temple with the roof falling in (6). For final reproduction (7), I selected a pale blue as the second color, to recall the color of the Greek flag.

1

2

4

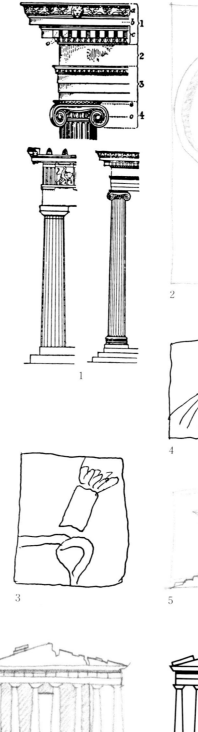

3

5

6

7

HOSTAGES IN IRAN

December 10, 1979

THIS SYMBOL was developed when the American hostages were first taken captive in Iran, and many different stories were needed to provide background to the event. Because of the timing and seriousness of the situation, it took a good deal of effort to arrive at a solution.

The first series of sketches (1) expressed the idea of the U.S. being attacked through a violation of its "territory"—the U.S. embassy in Tehran. Some of these sketches were more violent—as the U.S. flag or map being stabbed by a Moslem scimitar, or the flag being torn or going up in flames. One was highly symbolic—the word "Iran" imposed on a map of the U.S. This last idea was obviously not one I would use, but following my instincts, I jotted it down as a terse visual statement of the situation.

The second and third groups of sketches (2–3) pushed the ideas of applied force and political bal-

ance a bit further. There was also one attempt at drawing an arm with a white armband, such as people had begun wearing at the time; this practice quickly faded, however, and it was just as well that the idea wasn't used.

The last sketch of this series struck out in a new direction, depicting a confrontation between Iran and the U.S. as personified in the Ayatullah Khomeini and Uncle Sam. But at this point the idea was not developed.

By the time I started the fourth group of sketches (4), ideas were coming quickly; most of them had to do with the basic concept of "hostages." From news pictures of blindfolded and bound prisoners came one series of images, and most were obvious. One image employed a time bomb, a blindfold, some stars and stripes, and a pair of manacled hands to spell "Iran," but this was much too complicated, and, besides, it was the U.S.—not Iran—that was being held hostage.

At this point, I reviewed the whole lot and be-

1

2

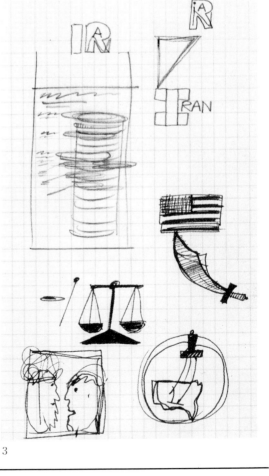

3

came interested in the sketch from the third group showing the Ayatullah and Uncle Sam. After all, once the initial outrage had passed, the two sides would have to come to some resolution. I began to notice the similarities between the two figures: both had beards and wore distinctive headgear, half of which could be as easily recognized as the whole. In a quick drawing (5), I established that the two "faces" might indeed be combined.

In three further trials (6), I worked out how the actual division between the two faces could be effected. The first of these three was rejected as being entirely too tame: it could have indicated some trade or cultural agreement between the two nations; similarly, the second indicated separation but not hostility. I finally settled on a ragged line that, by seeming to tear the face apart, would suggest the tension in the situation.

The final drawing (7) was constructed with templates and left the dividing space slightly larger at the top to enhance the idea of a tearing image.

5

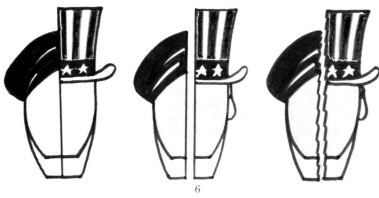

6

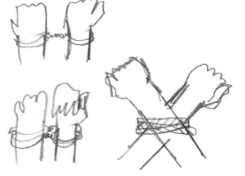

7

4

23

THE MIDDLE EAST
WAR IN THE GULF
October 27, 1980

IN ASSIGNING a cover illustration for an issue spotlighting the Iran–Iraq war, I prepared some sketches for a cover image to be painted by illustrator Daniel Maffia: an exploding oil barrel with the split between the two pieces taking the shape of the Persian Gulf (1). These sketches also became the basis for a symbol to connect the stories inside.

Most people may not have recognized that shape, but it really wasn't necessary to the success of the symbol: clearly, the war was about oil. Besides, the symbol was running with a large headline, as was the cover painting.

In preparing the symbol, I made another sketch of the oil barrel at 175 percent reproduction size to help visualize its orientation in space; from this I prepared the drawing (2) on which I based the final art (3).

1

2   3

ATTACK—AND FALLOUT

June 22, 1981

IN A SURPRISE move that shocked the world, Israeli Prime Minister Menachem Begin ordered the bombing of Iraq's nearly completed, French-built Tammuz 1 nuclear-research reactor. In following the logic that one of its deadliest foes would soon be making nuclear weapons, Israel had taken international law into its own hands, increased its isolation, strained relations with allies (including the U.S.), and raised another obstacle to securing peace in the Middle East.

To link the stories discussing these facets of the event, I developed a symbol that straightforwardly depicted the destruction of the reactor in the form of a large red "X."

The "X" was developed first (1–2), using a large brush dipped in black ink to draw bold swashes. Because the ink was wet and very messy, I worked on the floor of my office during this phase, drawing figures as wide as six and eight inches, in order to get a sense of strength and boldness. Then I lifted and tilted the paper so as to let the ink dribble a bit. From these sketches, of which two are shown here, I selected the one most dramatically pleasing (2).

The reactor, which was drawn from a photo reference (3), was actually somewhat disappointing: it was not in itself a symbol, nor was it visually interesting. At this point, I considered drawing some better-known object to indicate the reactor, but the Iraqi model was being shown on the cover and inside the issue, and it seemed only proper that it should be used.

By tracing the building and filling in the shadow areas, I was able to develop an image of a reactor building with a softly domed top, and although the form is all but obliterated by the large red "X," enough remains for the reader to recognize it as the building on the issue's cover.

1

2

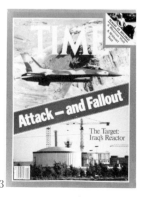

3

THE PALESTINIAN MASSACRE

October 4, 1982

THE WORLD WAS in shock. For two days or more, Israeli-backed Lebanese Christian militiamen roamed through the adjoining Palestinian camps known as Sabra and Shatila, just south of Beirut, brutally murdering men, women, and children. The bloodbath had caused great anguish among Israeli dignitaries and had severely strained U.S.–Israeli relations.

My first idea for a symbol to connect *Time* coverage of these stories was an attempt to picture Israel as the cause of bloodshed (1). However, the message was too strong, and the use of the Star of David could have been construed as indicating a massacre of Jews. Then I began to see the events as a people being wiped out, which I tried to depict by drawing an "X" through a face. But this symbol wasn't right, either.

As our photo coverage began to come in and I looked at the images of so many helpless people holding up their hands, another symbol idea began to take form: a forearm saying both "Help! and "Stop!"—an arm red with blood, or with blood trickling down it (2). However, after seeing photos of the horror and experiencing great revulsion, I found the symbol too loaded with emotion. To soften the feeling, I tried using an entire figure with arms upraised, but to show just one man or a woman and child would not clearly represent all parts of the story (3). Besides, the pictures that were to run with the story told clearly enough who the victims were.

Finally, I went back to the image of the upraised arm, and after devising the right shape, I drew two versions with clipped fingertips, the stark edges of which helped to convey a feeling of terror (4). By adapting the diamond shape and dotted background of two earlier sketches, I finally placed the red hand against a black backdrop with drop-out "bullet holes" in a random pattern. My idea complete, I did a tracing of the final drawing and prepared the symbol for reproduction.

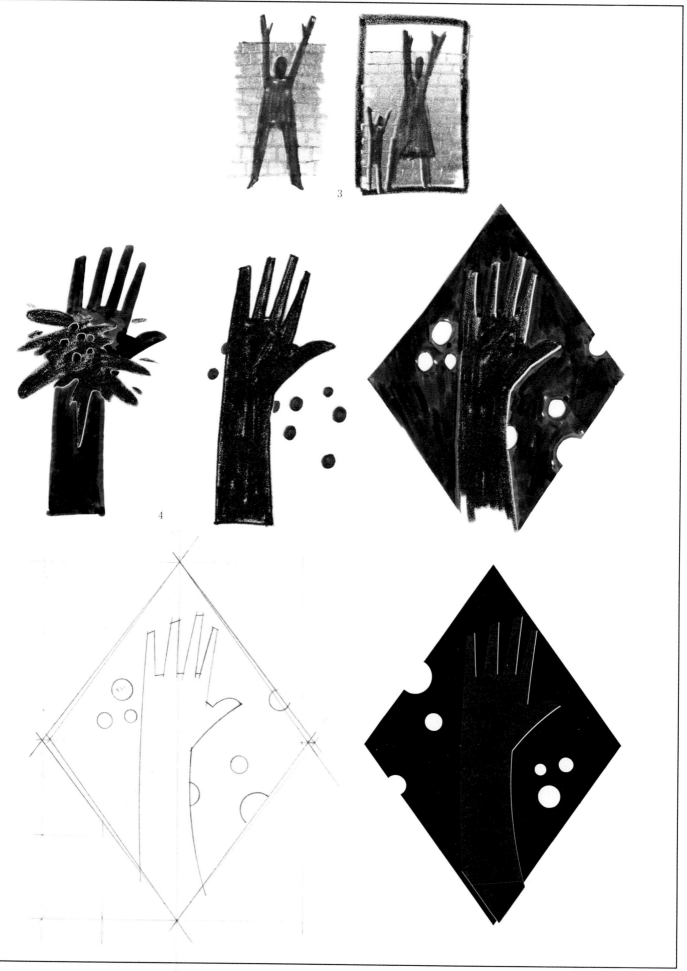

3

4

LOOKING FOR LIBYA'S HIT TEAMS
December 21, 1981

THE INDIVIDUAL reports were weak, but taken together, they had the strength of a warning. During the course of a few weeks, more than a dozen U.S. Government informants had tendered separate but supporting stories that Libyan leader Muammar Gaddafi had dispatched a number of "hit teams" to assassinate President Ronald Reagan and other top American politicos.

Gaddafi predictably denied the whole thing, and even some highly placed members of the Administration had their doubts. There was no hard evidence—only "sufficient reason to believe." This confusing and contradictory state of affairs, and how the Government intended to deal with it, became the focus of a special report in *Time*.

My first idea for a "hit team" symbol was to superimpose a commando-style rifle on a drop of blood (1). But the sketch seemed to convey that some sort of murder or violence had already taken place. There was in the image a finality that really wasn't present in the situation.

I needed to convey the uncertainty and skepticism surrounding the events, and the best way seemed to be with the addition of a question mark, which I mentally substituted for the drop of blood. Convinced the idea would work, I went about scaling up the repro size for a working drawing (2).

Here the rifle did not readily conform to the shape of the question mark; yet, because each element had a strong silhouette of its own, they worked successfully together. To impart a bit more visual unity, however, I drew the magazine of the rifle to the same curve as that of the question mark.

LIBYA'S HIT TEAMS

The Specter Of Terrorism

Colonel Muammar Gaddafi

1

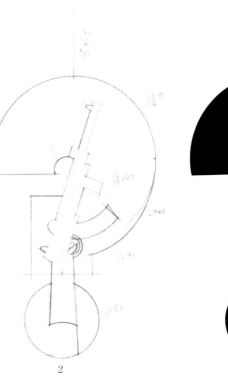

2

MIDDLE EAST TROUBLE SPOT

November 21, 1983

IT WAS A SHOWDOWN in the Middle East. U.S. warships arrived off the coast of Lebanon; Israel and Syria called up their reservists; warring Palestinian factions confronted one another in Tripoli; and Palestinian Liberation Organization leader Yasser Arafat faced the gravest challenge to his authority in the history of his career.

In some ways, this sort of symbol is from the start the least successful one can attempt. Because it has to embrace so many concepts, the image by necessity becomes terribly generalized. In this instance, it was the end of the week, and I found myself cornered: the magazine was going to press and needed a symbol.

At that point, the only possible solution I could see was the idea of a "trouble spot." I had used a similar solution in describing a series of conflicts in Central America; I had learned that the best way to handle this kind of problem is to devise a way to say, "This is the area."

For the Middle East trouble spot, I simply applied a press-on dot to a picture of the earth. Behind it I added a graduated tone pattern in the ocean areas of the globe to suggest the earth's roundness; this was printed blue. Land masses were run solid black and the trouble spot itself was bright red.

WATERGATE: Ten Years After

June 14, 1982

 FOR A DESIGNER who is British by birth and wasn't living in the U.S. at the time of the Watergate scandal, designing a symbol to accompany a series of articles marking the tenth anniversary of that event posed a unique challenge. Most British observers had reacted to the Watergate incident with a sense of surprise and disappointment. For me, the scandal had also provoked, for the first time, a genuine interest in American politics. But how did my feelings as a Briton compare with the feelings of Americans who had experienced the crisis firsthand?

To find out, I chatted informally with my American co-workers at *Time*. To my dismay, I found that while many of my colleagues had strong feelings about Watergate, emotional reactions were not that helpful in visualizing the events or their aftermath. Ultimately, I decided to develop a symbol from the events themselves, rather than from their emotionally charged atmosphere.

My first inclination was to draw a caricature of Richard Nixon, placing emphasis on the former President's shadowy growth of beard (1). However, I quickly abandoned this idea and began working on sketches that took their direction from the notion of looking and listening. These sketches (2–6) involved that well-known symbol for peeping and spying—the keyhole.

My first attempt was straightforward: an eye and a keyhole (2). However, since Watergate involved electronic eavesdropping, I decided to try detailing some evidence of that fact. To picture recording tapes, I reasoned, would be awkward: the uncoiling tapes would be difficult for the reader to distinguish from snakes or spaghetti or other tangling, linear forms. Thus, I chose to link a simple earphone image with the keyhole (3).

But the keyhole shape itself posed some problems. When executed as a solid-black form, it took on the appearance of a head upon which the earphones were placed. I tried experimenting with the illusion of three-dimensional space (4–6) before I hit upon a sketch I was happy with (6).

The final execution was achieved by using a fold-over tracing technique. Half the image was traced first (7). The tracing paper was then folded so that the mirror image could be traced. The result is a tightly drawn, perfectly symmetrical solution with a hardness of line that is particularly suited to the technological aspects of the Watergate crisis.

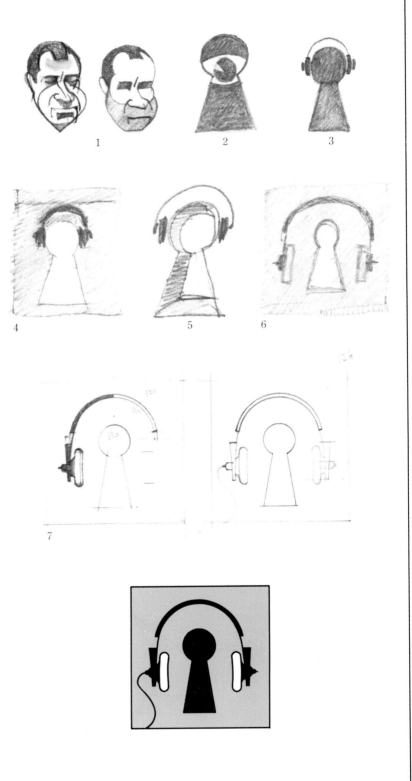

THE LENNON MURDER

December 22, 1980

ON A CERTAIN Monday evening in December of 1980, my wife and I were enjoying a leisurely dinner with artist Robert Grossman in a neighborhood restaurant. About halfway through the meal, someone noticed that the piped-in music we'd been hearing all evening had been exclusively Beatles' tunes. It wasn't until we reached home later that night that we learned former Beatle John Lennon had been killed just across town as we dined.

At the time of the shooting, the *Time* editors were already planning a story on violence in America, and we had started to think of a cover based on an image of guns. Not knowing at first the full impact of Lennon's death, the editors decided to turn the violence article into a theme issue that would also report on the killing. A cover was designed using a photo of a handgun and a portrait of Lennon by Daniel Maffia. However, by the week's end, the world reaction to the death of the Beatle had become so powerful that this story took precedence, and the portrait became the whole cover.

Thus, like the initial cover solution, the first symbols developed for this issue tried to connect two ideas—violence and a particular murder. However, neither a straightforward image of a gun (1), derived from photo reference, nor an image of Lennon's face drawn in half-shadow (2) proved adequate. By combining these two images on a shield-like device suggesting Lennon's face (3), a seemingly ideal solution was reached (4).

By press time, however, it became evident that the double-edged message of this design wasn't necessary: the portrait cover was in place, the stories being run quite graphic, and the accompanying visuals revealing. Moreover, the editorial thrust was now more that of an obituary for a Beatle than a journalistic treatment of violence.

Public reaction indicated that Lennon could not be separated easily from his music, and his instrument—the electric guitar—became the obvious base for the final solution (5).

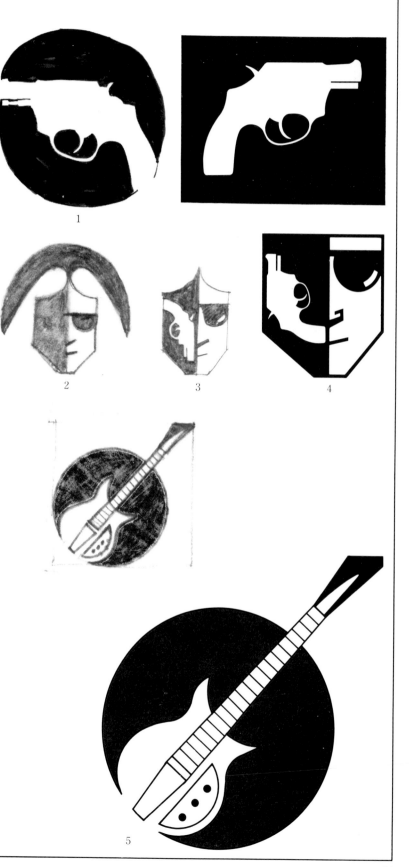

BUSTED: The John De Lorean Story
November 1, 1982

DISPASSIONATE reporting of arrests and incarcerations is the newsman's stock-in-trade. But when the accused is a well-known jetsetter and prominent American businessman, and the alleged offense involves 50 million dollars' worth of cocaine, passions are likely to run high.

Such was the case in reporting the arrest of John De Lorean, the American car-builder who, after a seven-month federal investigation, was arrested for trying to save his failing automotive business by pumping it full of drug-based profits. And, in designing a symbol to link together two stories about the case, my task was much like that of a *Time* reporter: to represent the facts without emotion, and to imply neither innocence nor guilt.

After considering the nature of De Lorean's business, my first instinct was to adapt straightforwardness of a typical American road sign to represent some aspect of the case—a sign meaning "Turn Ahead," for example, could be turned on its side to suggest a downturn in De Lorean's luck (1); the familiar "Stop" sign might mean that his purportedly illegal activities had been halted (2). But, in an effort to get beyond the obvious, I also tried two other ideas—one of a U.S. dollar sign whose vertical bar was formed by a straw, such as one might use to sniff cocaine (3), and one of the gull-

1   2

3

6

winged De Lorean automobile (4). Neither these two ideas nor the road signs seemed on target. In looking at the sketches, however, I had a hunch that the car would carry me to the ideal solution.

I was already using a side view of the automobile (5) in a chart appearing elsewhere in the coverage. Feeling my way, I sketched a back view of the car inside the international symbol for "Prohibited" (6). Now, however, I felt the image had become too strong and that the stories' underlying message was not so much one of crime and punishment but one of a car company in trouble. I decided to look at some photographs of the De Lorean automobile (7–8) for inspiration.

The stainless-steel De Lorean, with its gull-wing doors, sleek profile, and futuristic rear spoilers, it seemed, would not be easy to reduce to a symbol—especially one within the language of standard road signs. Then, by chance, I noticed, among the group of Letraset traffic signs I'd been using as reference, a symbol showing the rear of a car in a skid (9). It took but a short leap of imagination to turn "Slippery When Wet" into "Car Company in Trouble." I redrew the sign, incorporating a simplified version of the De Lorean car's distinctive rear end, and had a symbol (10) that was both distinctive and dispassionate.

5

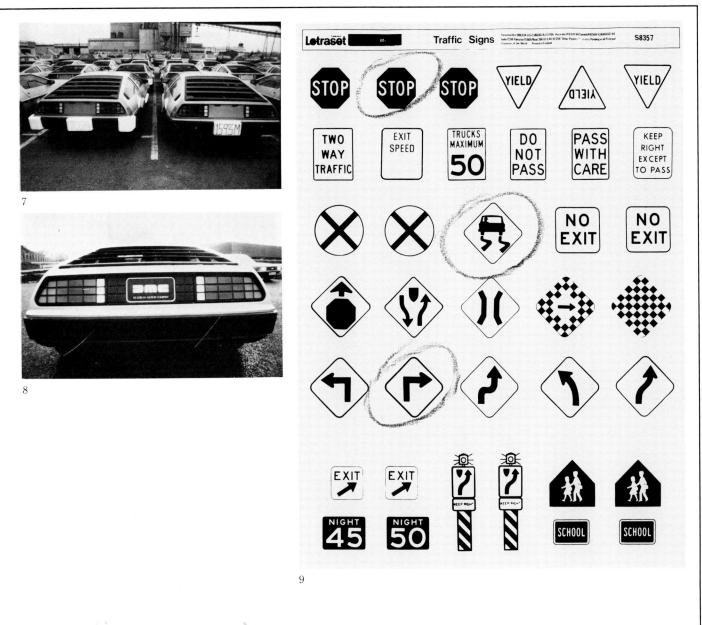

7

8

9

10

CRIME
VIOLENT CRIME

March 23, 1981

THREE MONTHS after the death of John Lennon (see page 31), *Time* ran its special report on "The Curse of Violent Crime" in America. And, like many other *Time* story symbols, the one for this report was inspired by the cover art and its strikingly graphic message.

Although we had commissioned a cover for the subject of violence from a different artist at the time of the Lennon shooting, another cover (1) was developed for this special issue. Painted by Marshall Arisman, the gruesomely powerful image of a deathmask-like face and a hand clutching a gun delivered an obvious message: violent crime in America really meant the proliferation of handguns and their involvement in the criminal loss of life and property.

Thus, a hand clutching a pistol was all that was necessary to continue the message inside. A couple of sketches (2) to work out the color, and it was on to a tight drawing and the final art (3–4).

In addition to appearing with the stories on violence, the symbol was used to highlight a letter from the publisher on the contents page.

Incidentally, another set of symbols (5) was designed for this issue, to indicate four types of violent crime: a coffin for murder; a hand with the symbol for "female" to represent rape; a money sack for robbery; and a hand with a knife for assault. The figures appeared on a map showing the dozen deadliest cities in the U.S.; the map was shaped like a burglar's mask, complete with cold, staring eyes (6).

1

2

3

4

MARCH 23, 1981   Vol. 117 No. 12

TIME

THE WEEKLY NEWSMAGAZINE

A Letter from the Publisher

The curse of violent crime has touched many American families, including our own. A surprising number of the TIME staff members who worked on this week's cover stories have themselves recently been victims of crimes. Senior Writer Ed Magnuson, who wrote the main story, was mugged at knifepoint as he put the key in the lock of his front door earlier this year. He lost $32 and his credit cards. A few months before that, Magnuson's apartment was burglarized. "The only evidence they left behind was a pair of shoes," he says. "They weren't even my size." Associate Editor John Leo, who wrote the assessment of crime's impact on American society, is a two-time burglary victim. Says he: "All U.S. cities are in danger of becoming unlivable. For a parent, the fear for your children is never very far from your mind."

Correspondent David Jackson awoke early one morning in his Chicago apartment to find a robber pointing a gun at him. The man took $5 and fled. Says Jackson: "Despite all the stories I had done about truly violent crimes, I was still unprepared for the clammy, hand-trembling fear that comes with being a victim." After a neighbor was brutally murdered in his Manhattan apartment building, Correspondent Robert Geline agreed to assist in the investigation. He was hypnotized by police in order to help him recall details of the crime. Says Geline sadly: "Eight months later the murder remains unsolved." Last month TIME's Marc Levinson had his Atlanta home broken into on two consecutive weekends. "I was not at home either time," says Levinson. "But I felt the anger and true sense of violation that come when someone has ransacked your property."

Last week Deputy Art Director Irene Ramp, who was working on the presentation of this week's cover stories, was the only customer in a Manhattan clothing store when two men walked in, drew pistols and demanded money from the cashier. Ramp remained silent in the dressing room, where she had been trying on a shirt, until the men had made their getaway with about $300. "If I had surprised them, anything could have happened," she says. Ramp emerged from the ordeal unscathed—but $25 poorer: "After watching the whole thing, I felt obliged to buy the shirt." Assistant Picture Editor Sue Considine, who gathered the photos that accompany the cover stories, lost $120 from her pocketbook in a Greenwich Village restaurant. Says she: "Now I know to keep it on my lap."

The most frightening thing, perhaps, is that it has all become so commonplace. But one crime, certainly, has left a lasting scar of frustration and loss on the entire staff. TIME Photographer Paul Keating was shot to death on a Manhattan street last year as he attempted to stop a mugging.

John A. Meyers

Index

TIME (ISSN 0040-781X) is published weekly at the subscription price of $35 per year, by Time Inc., 3435 Wilshire Blvd., Los Angeles, CA 90010. Principal office: Rockefeller Center, New York, N.Y. 10020. J. Richard Munro, President; J. Winston Fowlkes, Treasurer; Charles B. Bear, Secretary. Second class postage paid at Los Angeles, CA, and at additional mailing offices. Vol. 117 No. 12 © 1981 Time Inc. All rights reserved. Reproduction in whole or in part without written permission is prohibited. TIME and the Red Border Design are protected through trademark registration in the United States and in the foreign countries where TIME magazine circulates. POSTMASTER: Send address changes to TIME, Time-Life Building, 541 N. Fairbanks Court, Chicago, Il 60611.

5

THE DEADLY DOZEN
How they rank by type of crime

Murder · Rape · Assault · Robbery

Cleveland · Boston · Detroit · New York · San Francisco · Baltimore · Los Angeles · Washington · Dallas · Houston · New Orleans · St. Louis

Source: A survey of the 25 largest cities for the first six months of 1980, done by the Citizens Crime Commission of New York

TIME Charts by Nigel Holmes

6

35

THE REAGAN SHOOTING
April 13, 1981

JUST THREE WEEKS after *Time*'s special report on violence, an assassination attempt was made on President Ronald Reagan. The weapon—an ordinary "Saturday night special"—was a natural choice for a symbol to connect an unusually large number of stories on different aspects of the event: an interview with Mrs. Reagan, a look at the Secret Service, a medical feature on the President, and stories about the would-be assassin and the people caught in the crossfire. The coverage ended with an impassioned editorial in favor of banning handguns.

The symbol demanded little development. From a photo of a similar weapon, a solid black silhouette was made; this was placed against a red background comprising an "explosive" shape. The symbol was run large with the publisher's opening essay, then reduced to link the various stories inside.

CRIME
THE SHOOTING OF THE POPE
May 25, 1981

 THE THIRD IN a series of violent attacks on public figures, the attempt to assassinate Pope John Paul II shocked the world. Here, the surprising aspect was neither the weapon nor the violence, but the target of the attack itself. A man of God simply is not as likely to be murdered as a president or even a rock star.

In considering an appropriate symbol, a number of images came to mind, with bullet holes in the Papal Crown or a cross seeming most likely. Yet these seemed to suggest an attack on religion rather than on a person, and while religious factors may have been involved, no motive was known at the time.

The idea of the Pope as a target kept recurring. It was very much on people's minds, and the issue's opening editorial posed the question, "Why the Pope?" The image of a target would visually support the question, and there seemed to be no need for a bloodier, more violent symbol. A quick sketch of a bullet-riddled target (1) gave the right form to the idea, and there remained only the task of executing the finished art.

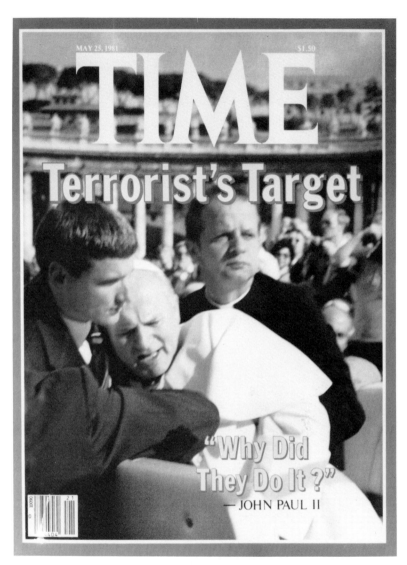

MAY 25, 1981 $1.50

TIME
Terrorist's Target

"Why Did They Do It?"
— JOHN PAUL II

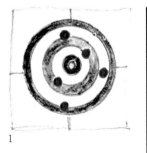

1

THE COLOMBIAN CONNECTION

January 29, 1979

FOR A REPORT on the Colombian marijuana trade, the obvious solution was a simplified marijuana leaf, adapted from Michael Doret's cover for the same issue.

Using the fold-over tracing technique (see page 30), I neatly lifted the shape and developed a symmetrical form (1). The symbol also appeared in a smaller version on a map accompanying the report.

1

BRITISH INDUSTRY
February 16, 1981

To ACCOMPANY a series of stories on Britain's labor problems, I again chose a play on the national flag as a symbol. The idea needed very little development, since—like the Stars and Stripes—the Union Jack is easily recognizable. To complete the image, I chose a traditional symbol for "industry"—the billowing smokestack (1). The latter is also particularly appropriate to the United Kingdom, where labor problems, despite modernization, are deep-rooted and long-standing.

By sketching out the British flag with a smokestack at one corner (2), I saw there could be no question to its meaning. Like the best symbols, it didn't need words to convey its content—although of course it would be supported by them in the pages of the magazine. After executing a working drawing to determine sizes and proportions (3), I proceeded to the finished art (4).

This symbol also tied in with the issue's cover, which was drawn by David Suter. Since this brilliant artist's work is heavily symbol-oriented and uses universally ingrained images with a "twist" in order to make a statement, the linking symbol was especially apt.

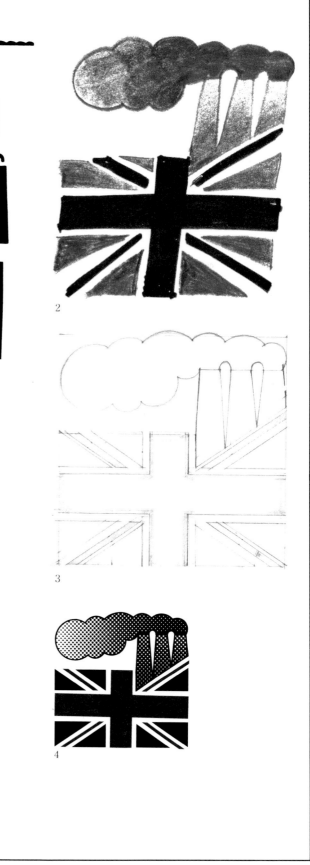

AMERICA SPEAKS TO THE WORLD
January 19, 1982

THE IDEA BEHIND this symbol was to convey the sense of America addressing, or presenting itself, to the world, and I started with the national flag. Like so many *Time* symbols, this one was developed in very little time as the magazine was going to press.

My first variation on the flag extended its red stripes and fanned them to suggest the spreading of information (1), but this was a bit too abstract. My next two attempts tried to include the world as represented by a globe, and the first of these (2) is especially interesting because it displays my unconscious world view: as an Englishman, I still tend to see the world with England near its center, prominently situated at the eastern edge of the North Atlantic. In the second attempt, I spun the globe a bit to reflect a more American viewpoint and added the U.S. in red with giant blue arrows leaping out of it (3), but I still wasn't satisfied.

Returning to the flag-and-arrow concept of my earliest attempt, I sketched three more variations. In the first (4), I removed the globe, leaving two circling arrows, but this might have been interpreted as the U.S. turning in on itself. The next design (5) pictured the arrows moving only horizontally, and in this figure lay the germ of the final solution. With the arrows viewed as moving east and west, the figure needed only the addition of northerly and southerly arms. Now, with a stylized flag at its center, the cruciform symbol (6) aptly suggested the U.S. speaking in all directions.

1

2

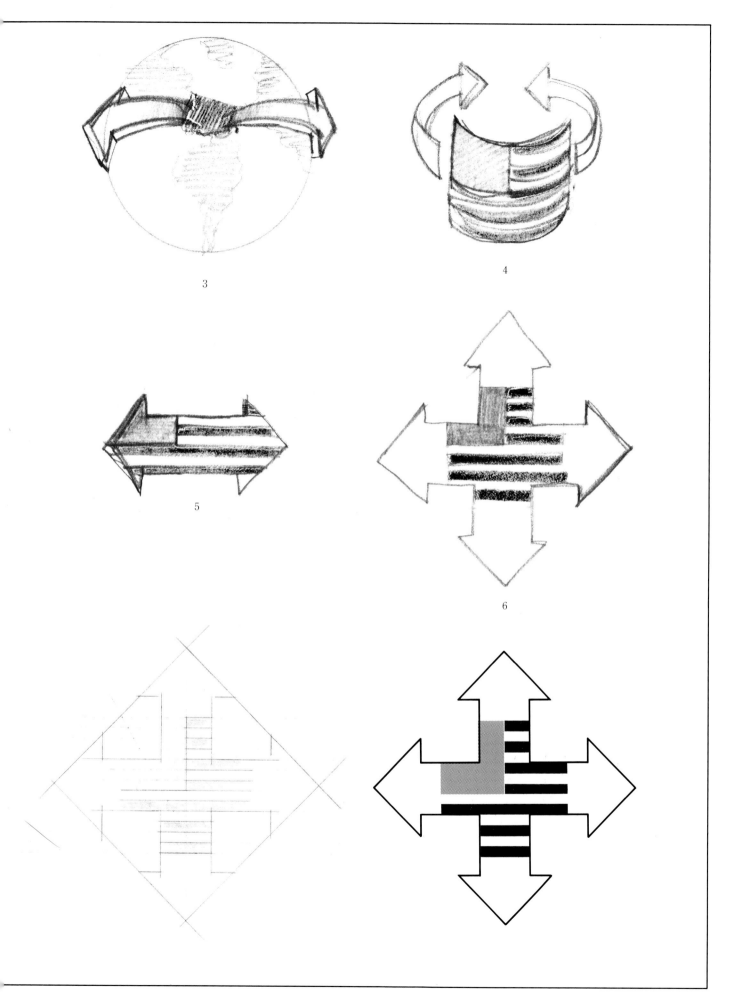

3

4

5

6

THINKING ABOUT THE UNTHINKABLE
March 29, 1982

IN AN AGE OF nuclear proliferation, Americans from Capitol Hill to Hollywood—and everywhere in between—were opening a national dialogue about how to control and cut back the nuclear stockpiles of the superpowers. The movement may have included some of the "peaceniks" from the days of the Viet Nam War, but by and large it was composed of a cross section of American culture, with individuals of all sorts of religious, political, and socio-economic stripes.

At this time, *Time* published a group of serious pieces on the idea of nuclear disarmament, and the layout was very carefully planned. The opening spread, which contained a think-piece about the unthinkable, focused on a four-column photo of an atomic fireball. The two remaining columns of text included space for a symbol that would tie all the stories together.

My first efforts reflected the idea of thinking, by using the mushroom cloud to fill the cranium of a talking head (1). But this figure appeared to be talking only to himself. My next attempt incorporated a second face and—in a variation of an old optical illusion—used the negative space between the two to create a mushroom-shaped cloud (2).

Still pushing toward the obvious, I thought it might be best to play it completely straight. I made two sketches to convey the idea of "dropping the

1

2

bomb" (3–4). Both featured the cloud form; in the second of the two, the cloud was quite stylized and contained a bomb in a nose-dive. But in light of the photograph that was to appear opposite the symbol on the opening spread, there seemed little point in using another mushroom-shaped cloud.

In the course of the various national discussions, there had been a lot of talk about "pushing the button," and in this phrase, I thought, lay a possible solution. I made a series of sketches showing a finger or hand doing just that (5), but they either showed too much of the hand or looked more like someone pressing a light switch. Only the second sketch in the series succinctly conveyed the idea, and it ultimately became the symbol we used (6).

This symbol with a finger about to press a red button seen in profile is one of my favorites. First, I like the details of the finger itself—the cuticle, the space below the clipped nail, the informal wrinkles at the knuckle. It's a very personal finger and eminently human.

In terms of context (7), I like the way the symbol works through the idea of causation: a finger pressing a button, left, setting off a nuclear blast, right. It's not often that *Time* runs a picture as large as this one, and paired with the small symbol, the effect is all the more dramatic: that such a small, human act could cause such horrible destruction.

3

4

TIME/MARCH 29, 1982

COVER STORIES

Thinking About The Unthinkable

Rising fears about the dangers of nuclear war

No army can stop an idea whose time has come.
—Victor Hugo

An idea whose moment may have arrived is sweeping the U.S.—for better or for worse. From the halls of Congress to Vermont hamlets to the posh living rooms of Beverly Hills, Americans are not only thinking about the unthinkable, they are opening a national dialogue on ways to control and reduce the awesome and frightening nuclear arsenals of the superpowers. This new awareness of the dangers of nuclear war cuts across traditional political boundaries. Advocates of a bilateral freeze on the development and deployment of nuclear weapons include some peacenik activists who led protests against U.S. involvement in the Viet Nam War a decade ago. But the new movement is far more broadly based; it includes more bishops than Berrigans, doctors and lawyers with impeccable Establishment credentials, archconservatives as well as diehard liberals, and such knowledgeable experts as retired Admiral Noel Gayler, former director of the supersecret National Security Agency, and former SALT II Negotiator Paul Warnke. Says Rabbi Alexander Schindler, head of the Union of American Hebrew Congregations: "Nuclear disarmament is going to become the central moral issue of the '80s, just as Viet Nam was in the '60s."

The central goal of the movement is to educate the public to the true horrors of what war would mean to the U.S. and the world today, and thereby put pressure on a hawkish Administration to negotiate a cutback in nuclear arms with the Soviet Union. Some of that prodding is already coming from Congress. Senators Edward Kennedy of Massachusetts and Mark Hatfield of Oregon two weeks ago introduced a resolution that calls for a freeze on the testing, production and further deployment of nuclear weapons by both the U.S. and the Soviet Union. The nonbinding measure has already attracted the support of 22 Senators and 150 Representatives.

That was not all. Republican Charles McC. Mathias of Maryland last week introduced another Senate resolution calling upon the President to "immediately invite" the Soviets to negotiations on strategic arms and the proliferation of nuclear weapons and technology. Mathias charged that the Administration was guilty of a "grievous failure" for not having initiated such negotiations. "Nothing less than the future of mankind is at stake," he said.

The resolutions on Capitol Hill are the small tip of a very large iceberg. In part, the Senators who favor the motions are responding to an unprecedented flood of teach-ins, referendums, legislative proposals, letter-writing campaigns, petitions, and books addressing the peril of nuclear war. The groups involved in the movement include such longtime disarmament organizations as SANE and the Union of Concerned Scientists. But with them are a host of fledgling organizations: Physicians for Social Responsibility, International Physicians for the Prevention of Nuclear War, the Lawyers Alliance for Nuclear Arms Control, the Business Alert to Nuclear War, Artists for Survival. The St. Louis-based National Clearinghouse for the Nuclear Weapons Freeze Campaign, founded last December, estimates that 20,000 volunteers are now involved in the crusade nationwide.

Although its hard-cover publication by Alfred A. Knopf will not occur until April, one of the most talked-about books of the year is Jonathan Schell's *The Fate of the World.* First published in *The New Yorker* last month, it is an impassioned argument that nuclear weapons have made war obsolete and world government imperative. Astonishingly, some 40 new books on nuclear issues are scheduled to be published before the end of this year. Pocket Books is rushing into bookstores with 100,000 copies of *Nuclear War: What's in It for You?,* a paperback primer on the subject, written by Roger Molander, founder of

Fireball of an H-bomb explosion rises over Bikini Atoll after a 1956 test blast

10

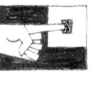

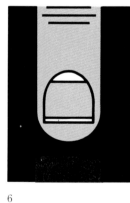

5

6

HEAVYWEIGHT HITS
June 14, 1982

SUMMER WAS BLOOMING; *Rocky III* brought Sylvester Stallone back to the silver screen, Gerry Cooney was challenging heavyweight champ Larry Holmes in Las Vegas, and *Time* ran a kind of fun summer cover highlighting the two spectacular events.

Like the cover, the symbol for the stories inside had to tie together Hollywood and boxing. Fortunately, there are elements of boxing in Hollywood, and certainly many elements of Hollywood in boxing. But how to portray the two in one concept?

My first attempts (1–4) were far too literal in their efforts to combine filmstrips or movie cameras with boxing gloves; another idea placing the ropes of a boxing ring around a spotlight proved too abstract (5). But when I placed a figure in the spotlight (6), I knew I'd found a viable solution. The figure, with arms raised, could be an entertainer or, with rounded mitts, a boxer.

I tried two other versions of this idea (7), to test both round and square background shapes, and chose the round background because another symbol in the same issue of the magazine was using the square. These sketches employed both the ropes of the boxing ring and a figure with gloved hands; the hands had to be drawn oversized in order to be read when reduced. (In the final drawing, these bulb-like hands were as large as the figure's head.)

To prepare the concept for reproduction, I first made a color sketch (8) to work out the composition and color percentages: a black figure; a yellow circle of light on the floor; and a blue spotlight ray (which might better have been another color) for contrast with the yellow ellipse. Then, from a tracing of the sketch, I prepared the repro art with screen tints and overlays.

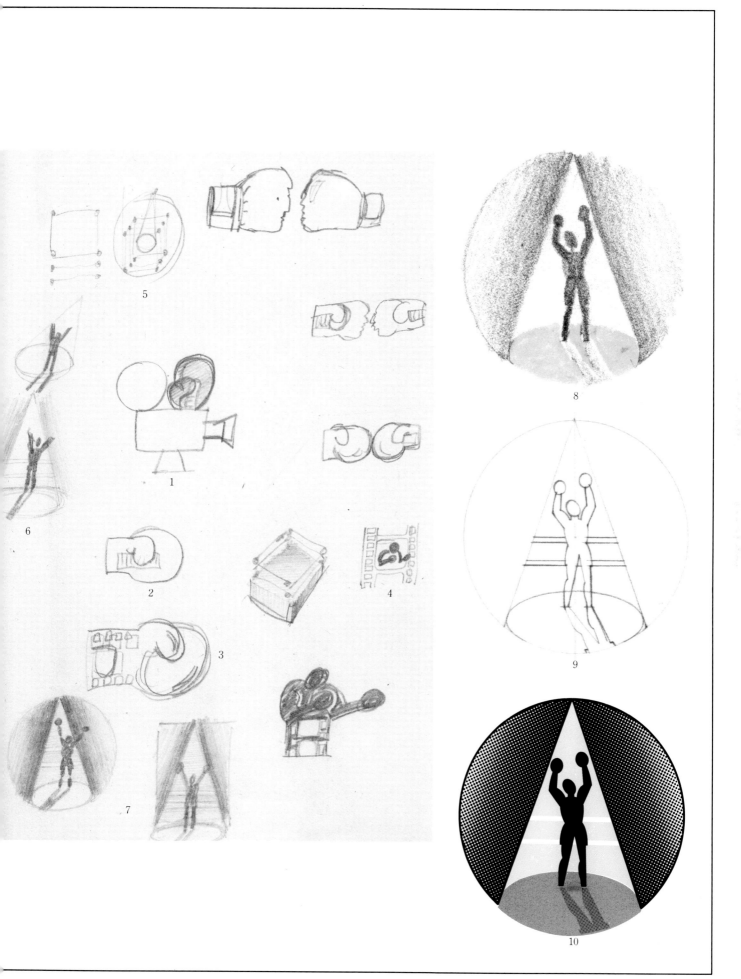

5

1

6

2

3

7

4

8

9

10

BROADWAY BLOCKBUSTERS

October 5, 1981

IT WAS A HAPPY time for the theater and theatergoers: Broadway (and off-Broadway) was booming with a number of successful shows, and the boom was epitomized by one show called *Nicholas Nickleby*, which provided a day at the theater for an admission price of one hundred dollars. Although the *Time* stories were pegged on the *Nickleby* phenomenon, they really addressed a broader resurgence of theater in America.

The obvious symbol for such a happy circumstance was the happy half of the well-known symbol for tragedy and comedy, here constructed with templates using the fold-over technique. It was printed in black and bright yellow to keep it light and happy.

Looking back, the symbol might just as well have been used for a story about the theatricality of ice-hockey goaltenders; as it was, the lively mask proved a fresh version of a well-tried symbol and the successful replaying of an image people already knew.

MICHAEL JACKSON: Pop Phenomenon
March 19, 1984

IN THE GLITTERY world of show business, celebrities often shield themselves from a curious public, and the more successful the personality, the greater the curiosity—and the tougher the shield.

In attempting to report upon rock phenomenon Michael Jackson, *Time* reporters were stonewalled by the recording artist as well as by his family, friends, and neighbors. A special issue on the artist was about to close with only a third-person Jackson cover story when the magazine's Los Angeles correspondent got an interview with the singer's parents—and a glimpse of the celebrity himself. This was a coup for the editors and a challenge to me: at the last minute, I had to develop a symbol to link the two stories.

The natural solution to my eye was a white glove: the singer never performs without one, and this along with a red jacket are already ersatz Jackson symbols among pop culture buffs (1). But *Time*'s editors, who more or less figure as Everyman in their decision making, were uneasy. After all, they were professionals and well beyond the age of rocking-and-rolling. If the "obvious" solution were lost to them, would it work for the man in the street?

Following their cue, I neatly moved from Jackson's hands to his feet. The singer's evolution as a show business personality had brought him renown as a dancer—especially since the release of his *Thriller* music-video. Jackson also had certain other qualities that I felt might be worth exploring—for example, his androgynous appearance, his winning smile, and his associations with show business. After a brainstorming session with the editors, I sat down to draw and produced a number of sketches, including some of the singer in a spotlight and of a curly haired boy with a lipstick smile (2–21). But none of these clicked, and I went home to sleep on it.

Next day, I tried again. This second session produced ideas along several tacks. The first, which I instinctively felt was probably the best way to go, focused on Jackson's dancing, which was peculiarly angular in style and might lend itself to a particular personality-oriented graphic. These color roughs were directly related to the dancing figures I had sketched the day before and incorporated other ideas as well—the singer's epauleted red jacket, for example, or music notes (27–31) in place of his

1

2   3

4   5   6

legs. Other ideas sketched during this session referred to recent Grammy ceremonials, where Jackson collected an unprecedented eight awards and where, after receiving the last one, he had removed the dark glasses he'd been wearing for the duration of the show (25–26). Also sketched here were a gold-star disc (24), music notes and microphones (22).

But at the end of all this exploration, the image of Jackson-the-Dancer remained supreme. The editors rejected any references to the Grammy awards as being out of the scope of the story, and the sunglasses incident they regarded as too vague. They agreed with me that the best solution was a dancer, and—now that they had read the copy for both stories—they asked me to include in the figure's costume one white glove.

From this point, it was a matter of refining the idea. I selected a pose from a picture appearing in a previous issue of *Time* with a story about the *Thriller* video and enlarged it to a workable size. Then I simplified the figure by tracing its legs with a ruler (to accentuate their angularity) and by reducing the jacket to one red shape (32). The addition of an electrified yellow background provided the finishing touch—and conveyed the tremendous energy of this talented young performer.

14

15

16

17

18

19

20

21

NIGEL HOLMES

24

22

25

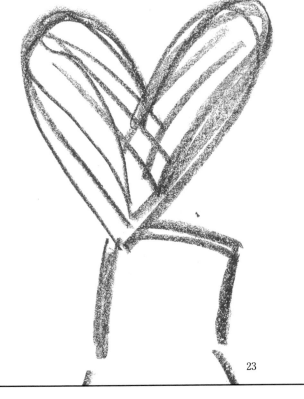

23

26

27

28

29

30

31

32

33

34

THE EUROPEAN ECONOMY

April 2, 1984

 THIS SYMBOL, which appeared in *Time*'s international editions, was developed to connect two stories about the European economy—one about Europe as a whole, the other about France.

My first idea (1) was to set a map of Europe into the French flag, but this image placed too much emphasis on the role of France. Similarly, the second solution (2), which made Europe seem to appear from behind the fluttering flag, was not appropriate. Then I tried a dual symbol comprised in the upper half of a composite of various European flags, and in the lower half by the French flag (3). I realized this image would be far too complicated to print, but it did lead me to the final solution: a flag of a united Europe (4).

By changing the colors in this design, I easily adapted it to each of the two story lines. For the one about Europe, the members of the European Economic Community were printed in blue; for the one on France, that country alone was printed in red. In both cases, the remaining land masses in the map were printed in a tint of black. Because blue was already being used, water portions of the map were printed in a wavy green banknote pattern.

4

1

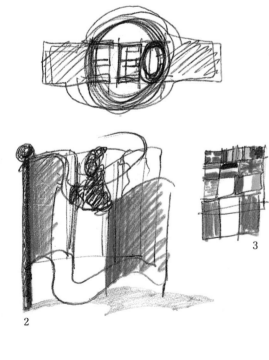

2

3

1984 OLYMPIC GAMES

FOR MANY AMERICANS, the quadrennial Olympic Games offer a unique opportunity to combine an avid love of athletic competition with a healthy patriotism. But in recent years, the Games have been marred too often by events rightly belonging to the political arena, and, at times, the politics surrounding the Games has affected *Time*'s treatment of them.

WINTER GAMES

January 30 and February 13, 1984

 BECAUSE OF the success of American athletes during the previous Winter Games (most notably the American defeat of the Russian ice hockey team), and because the U.S. once again had many strong contestants, as the 1984 Winter Olympiad approached, American enthusiasm was high.

Work on *Time*'s Olympic coverage was started early, and by the time I started thinking about a symbol for the Winter Games, special section art director Tom Bentkowski had already set aside space for it on the first page of the Olympics section. Initial coverage was to include a report on Sarajevo, Yugoslavia, scene of the winter events, with other stories to run before and during the Games.

With a review of editorial needs, it seemed that a single symbol meaning "Winter Olympics" might not meet the needs of some of the other stories, especially those on the U.S. team and its favored skiers and skaters. And, while most *Time* symbols connect different strands of the same story within one issue of the magazine, here the solution would have to function with coverage that was both broad and specific and comprised of different sections to be spread over several issues.

Taking a cue from the opening spread, which prominently pictured the village of Sarajevo nestled against a mountainside, I began a series of sketches that were both conceptual and pictorial (1). The most compelling feature of the Sarajevo geography was its mountainous terrain, and this became the basis for a general Winter Olympics symbol. Complete with snow-capped peaks, the mountains then became the backdrop for the rest of the symbol series, just as they were the backdrop for the Games themselves. In these symbols, the horizon line remained constant, as did the colors—a blue background of sky, a snowy white middle ground, and highlight colors of red and black. Wherever convenient, the interlocking Olympic rings, official symbol of the Olympics, were dropped out. From these first sketches, it was a few simple steps to tracings (2) and finished art (3).

The final symbols have the coherence and scale of a set of special issue U.S. postage stamps, and are no less appealing.

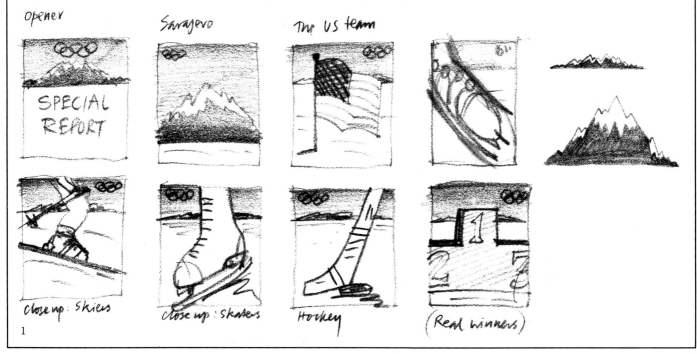

1

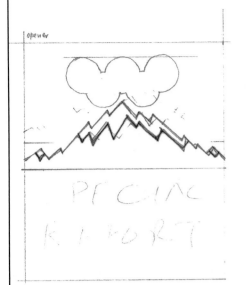

opener

sarajevo

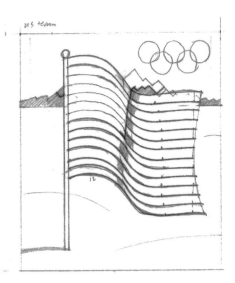

us team

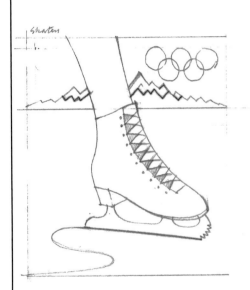

skaters

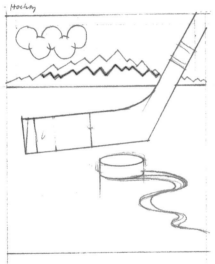

Hockey

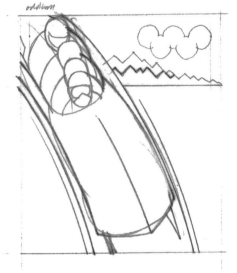

bobsled

skiers

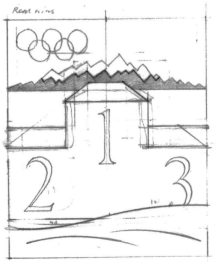

Reat wins

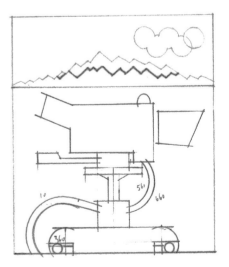

3

SUMMER GAMES
May-August, 1984

FOR THE 1984 Summer Olympics, the third to be held in the U.S., we planned a huge special issue. On the morning of the day the runner bearing the Olympic torch arrived in New York City, a staff meeting was called to make certain final decisions. A few hours later, the Russians pulled out of the Games, and word came down that the special issue was to be scrapped. It was no small irony that as I looked crestfallen into the Avenue of the Americas from my 25th floor office in Rockefeller Center, I glimpsed the Olympic torch passing by, still held high.

By the time this decision had been made, both art and editorial staffs had already worked many hard hours in developing the special issue. Always a momentous occasion for *Time*, special "one-subject" issues had been published only twice before. In addition, I had a good deal of personal feeling for the Games and had done a lot of work in connection with the 1972 and 1976 Olympics while with the London *Radio Times*. Now I was in America, where the Games were being held, working for a big American news magazine. The excitement had been real, but since Russia had pulled out, the whole tenor of the Olympics had changed.

Another staff meeting determined that all of our enthusiasm and effort should not be lost. The features already in preparation for the special issue would be run one or more to an issue, starting in May, until a special Olympics report appeared in the July 30 issue. Although greatly curtailed, on some level at least the project had been saved.

While the special issue would no doubt have called for a number of symbols, the current situation did not. The revised Olympic coverage, which included stories on such loosely linked issues as traffic problems in Los Angeles, sports medicine,

politics, fund-raising, and computers, needed a single unifying image.

In reviewing Olympic treatment done by various designers through the years, two aspects of the problem became apparent. The first was how to utilize the Olympic symbol in a uniquely American way; the second, how to make its long, narrow shape work visually in the pages of the magazine. The first sketches (1) tackled these problems directly by trying to incorporate the rings with something that uniquely meant "America" or "Los Angeles"—hence, variations on the Hollywood sign, the U.S. flag, and a movie camera. Then, in an attempt to cut through to essentials, I began experimenting with the rings themselves (2) which I ultimately cropped and placed in a square.

But the square shape seemed a bit clumsy with the breadth of linked, cropped rings. Then I recalled my work for the *Radio Times*, in which I devised a diamond-shaped frame for some sports symbols (see page 128–129). This shape I felt was particularly suited to the configurations of the rings and particularly strong in its own right: because type cannot be easily set around it, it creates its own space on the page.

In developing the symbol for presentation, I worked up both the square and the diamond versions (3–5). Since the symbol would be used some 30 times, it couldn't be too clever and would have to function without calling too much attention to itself. The presentation concepts, therefore, were essentially the same—the cropped Olympic rings, dropped out of a graduated blue sky (made from blue and black) and bordered by a rich red frame. The editors agreed with the forcefulness of the diamond shape, and our own 1984 Summer Olympic symbol was complete.

1

TIME
INCORPORATED

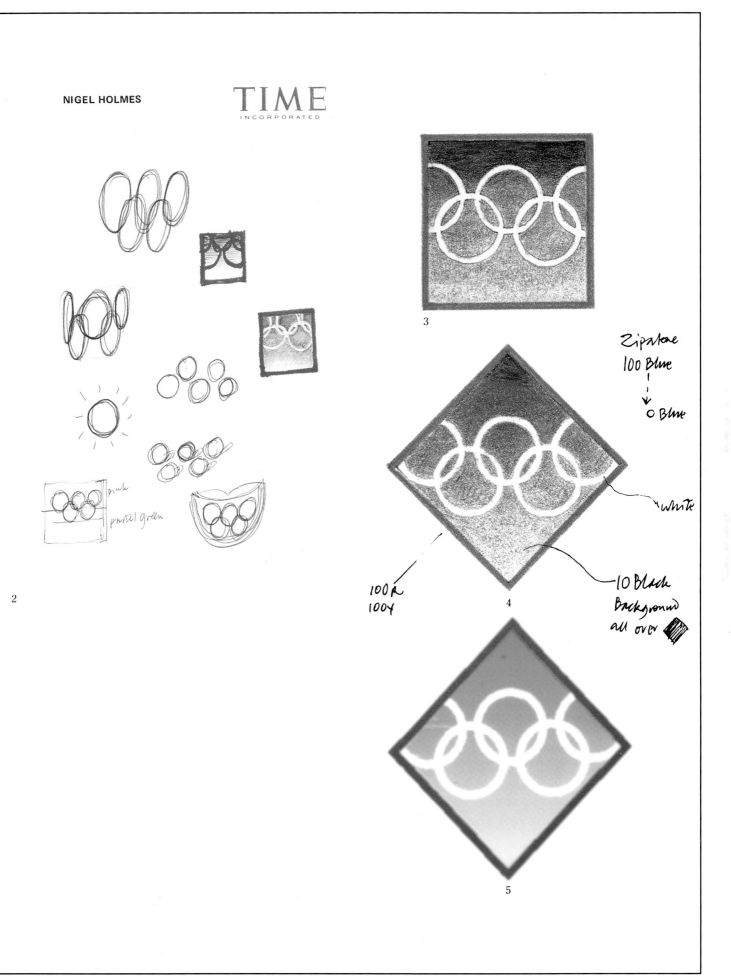

MEXICO'S POPULATION CRISIS

August 6, 1984

THE PRIME motivation for a group of articles on population growth and other urban problems was a world population conference held in Mexico City. However, a story on Mexico City itself had been in progress for some time.

With its population increasing at the rate of one million per year, Mexico's premier urban center had only 3.1 million inhabitants in 1950. By 1984, the number had climbed to 17 million and was expected to reach 26 million by the end of the century. With staggering problems of pollution, corruption, and overcrowding, the city's future looked bleak indeed.

With a burgeoning population at the root of the troubles, I set out trying to find a way to make a symbol that was uniquely Mexican. My first thoughts were disparate—a bright skull that could have been a Mexican tourist trinket (1); a group of silhouettes increasing in size (2); a styled Aztec pyramid beneath a black sky (3); a human figure comprised of other human figures (4).

Of these, the second two looked most promising, and I began experimenting to find a way to combine them into one symbol. At about this time, I remembered a sheet of printers' "bullets" (5) that had always reminded me of a sea of people; these it seemed might work with the pyramid to make a symbol.

In preparation I studied some paintings of Aztec pyramids and set the circles into the shape (6–15). Convinced it would work, I selected colors that, after a casual poll of the office, seemed best to indicate "Mexico." I placed a pyramid of black figures against a yellow-orange pyramid and

1

2

3

4

roughed in a backdrop of green, which might be seen as a polluted sky. Then I worked out the arrangement of dots (15, 16). The last sketch I showed to the editor, who liked it although he wasn't sure he understood it.

His doubt took me back to the drawing board. Although the symbol said Mexico, the stories altogether were of a broader nature. So I reduced the pyramid shape to a side detail (17) that would underplay the Mexican angle. However, the editor still had difficulty seeing the figures as people, and I began to experiment with more defined human shapes (18–21). These I ultimately felt were either too businesslike or too plebeian, and in either case too complicated. I went back to the bullets, which were straightforward and very abstract. To me, they would have been the ideal symbols for faces, and would have worked well in conjunction with a painting by Eugene Mihaesco that was appearing with the stories. But the circles alone did not lend themselves to color, which I felt bound to use.

Finally, I returned to the pyramid. To make the faces more detailed at this point would seem to clutter the composition, and when I met again with the editors to discuss the problem, suddenly everyone liked the symbol as it was (17). From it I did a tracing to work out the spacing of the figures within the pyramid, which had to be very precise (22). In the final art (23), the black faces do not indicate black people but all peoples of the world; the pyramid shape is not a true pyramid but a symbol for it.

As in many cases, the correctness of this solution was arrived at not by reason but by feeling my way toward it through development.

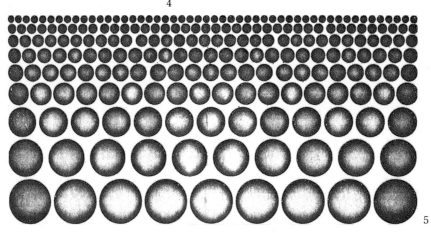

5

6

7

8

9

10

11

12

13

14

15

16

17

18

19

20

21

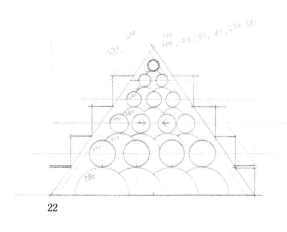
22

23

BEIRUT UNDER SIEGE

July 19, 1982

THE SECOND of a series of symbols pertaining to the continuing war in Lebanon was executed as U.S. and Israeli forces converged on Beirut in attempts to force withdrawal of P.L.O. troops. Here, my first idea employed well-known images for the three nations involved (1): two arrows, composed of parts of flags of the U.S. and Israel, coming together over one of the fabled cedars of Lebanon, which also appears on that country's flag.

But as the situation developed during that week, what became important was not the different sides involved, but what was happening to Beirut itself because of the conflict. In an attempt to convey the heavy damage to the city, I adapted the arrow forms as part of the negative space around a large red "X," which seemed to be encroaching upon the cedar tree (2–3). But the "X" implied that all of Lebanon was being destroyed, which really wasn't the situation. This symbol, therefore, was too strong.

By this time, we began receiving photo coverage of the seige of Beirut, and these pictures of a city on fire gave me the image I'd been looking for. My first sketch from the photographs gave equal emphasis to both cityscape and flames (4), but this was an unnecessary complication of the situation, which I decided could be conveyed by use of the flames alone. I drew two versions of this symbol (5, 6) before arriving at the right configuration.

The final version printed as a bright red flame against a blue-black background of billowing smoke (7).

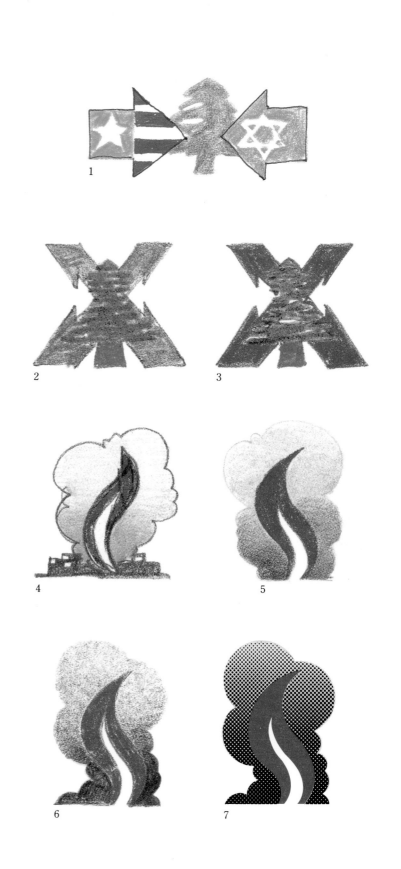

1

2

3

4

5

6

7

A WEEK AT WAR
June 28, 1982

THE CONNECTING symbol for this issue of *Time*, which dealt with wars in Lebanon and the Falkland Islands, was directly influenced by its cover art—or, more accurately, by the art that was supposed to have appeared on its cover.

When I received the assignment to design a symbol relating five different stories about these wars, artist Eugene Mihaesco was already at work on a cover illustration. But by the time Mihaesco submitted the finished work (1), the situation in Lebanon had worsened, and the painting seemed too light for the bleak picture of events. *Time*'s editors made the decision to use a typographically oriented cover (2), and moved Mihaesco's painting to the inside, where it appeared as the illustration for the lead article.

Throughout that week, I had been working on a war symbol that directly reflected my own sensibilities. Although the situation in Lebanon was extreme, as an Englishman my personal outrage was centered on the situation in the Falklands, where Britain was trying to reclaim her territory, and on my own passionate feelings as to the immorality of all war. My first ideas—which involved the typographic elements I eventually incorporated into the cover design—were simply a starting point from which I hoped to tie together the various war stories (3–13).

But as I worked and the wars raged, my feelings grew in intensity. I made more sketches, and these resonate with my outrage: strong pencil strokes, violent lines, and dynamic compositions fuse in a series of ideas—an angry face that is also a rolling tank, a broken bomb, two gun barrels "talking" to one another. While I knew these solutions weren't right for the magazine, I also realized the value of the exercise—to get beyond my own emotions and to channel the angry energy into ideas that might be useful later on.

Once it was moved inside, Mihaesco's painting became the obvious symbolic image. However, the very surface character of the image, which was powerful at a larger scale, would have been lost had the painting itself been used as a symbol, and the artist was not comfortable with reducing it for this purpose himself. So, it was left to me to stylize the dove-and-barrel into a symbol format (13–16).

1

2

3

4

5

6

7

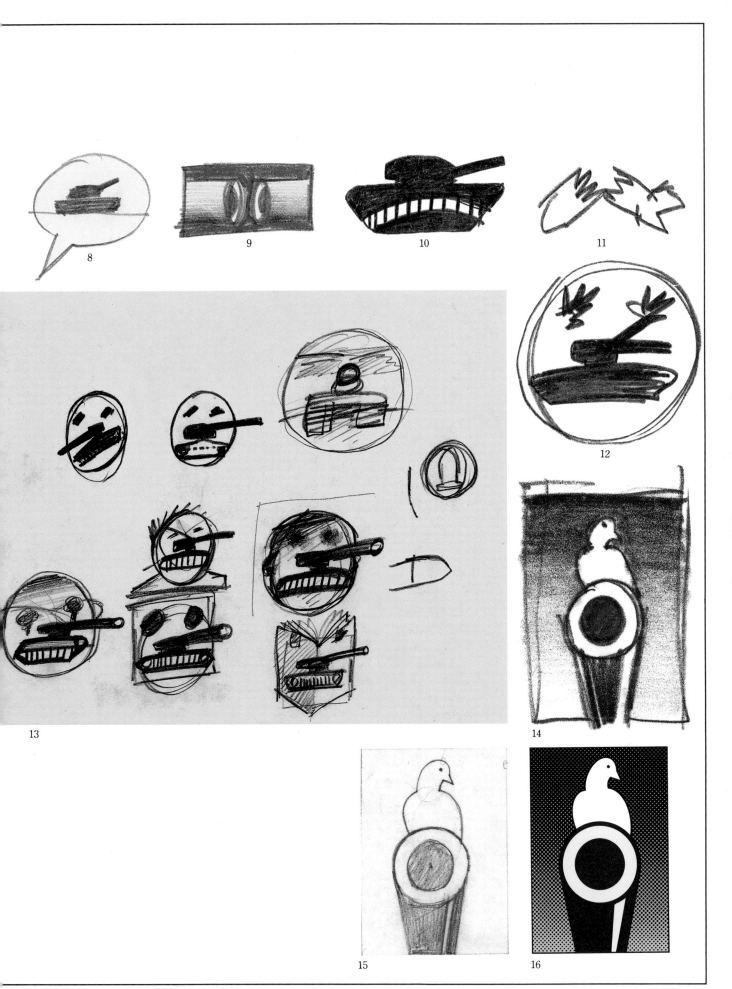

8

9

10

11

12

13

14

15

16

THE MARINES IN LEBANON
February 27, 1984

AFTER SPENDING some $120 million, sacrificing 265 U.S. servicemen and wounding another 134, and failing at both diplomatic and military efforts to hold together a crumbling Lebanese government, the U.S. Marines were pulling out of Lebanon. And once again, Americans were asking some belated questions: Should the Marines have been there in the first place? If so, should Reagan now be calling them back?

Here the focus of the story was on the Marines rather than the politics of the situation, and my attempts to find a symbol were all rooted in the image of a helmeted Marine. The first group of sketches (1–6) attempted to fit inside the helmet a cedar tree taken from the Lebanese flag. The first drawings were quite literal (2, 3); then the tree became a shape inside a helmet placed on a Marine's head. But this image was far too complicated. In addition, the tree might have been misconstrued as some sort of camouflage.

The next series attempted to locate the Marines in Lebanon. Here the face was retained from the previous sketches, and an American flag was pasted to the side of the helmet (7–11). But the flag was redundant: everyone knew the Marines were Americans, so it became a matter of developing a background for the helmeted figure. I felt the simpler, the better, and sketched three versions of a city skyline engulfed in an explosive shape.

The final version (12) seemed to evoke best the idea of the Marines in an explosive situation. The jagged red background is both strong and evocative; printed in shaded red over solid yellow, the shape becomes yellower and "hotter" as it reaches the flame-like tips, which contain no red at all.

From this last sketch I made a template tracing (13) for use in preparing repro art (14).

1

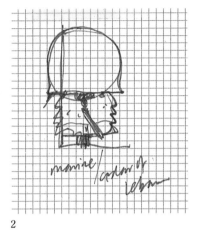

2

3

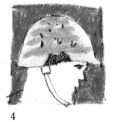

4

5

6

7

8

9

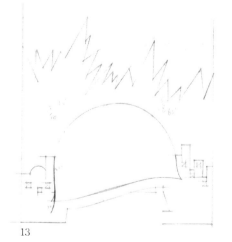

10

11

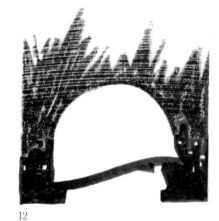

12

13

14

TWO MIDDLE EAST WARS
July 26, 1982

IN THE ISSUE following the one reporting the siege of Beirut (see page 61), there were two separate and continuing wars for which *Time* provided updated coverage—the war in Lebanon and the war in the Persian Gulf. As a first step in developing a symbol for these stories, I jotted down sketches of the flags of the nations involved (1). These I knew might be useful in symbol development by providing colors or other imagery.

The sketches that followed (2–6) dealt with the idea of one nation crossing boundaries and going into another: during the wars in question, Iran had entered Iraq, and Israel had gone into Lebanon. In both wars, the movement had resulted in explosive conflicts; hence, the symbol sketches were composed of arrows and explosive shapes, with colors derived from the flags of three of the four nations involved. But what developed here was a group of interesting shapes that in retrospect were too abstract—which is probably why I rejected them at the time.

My next idea (7) was in a different direction and of more literal imagery than that of the first series. Here, a tank is seen simultaneously attacking and being attacked. But this image was far too complicated.

By this time, *Time*'s editorial thinking had evolved to a point where it became important to deal with the fact that *people* were fighting these wars. In direct response to this consideration, I developed a symbol for a soldier, one that did not represent "army" in the abstract, but an individual (8). This, it seemed, would be the ideal solution; for, in picturing a situation as it develops from week to week, it is always best to avoid too many generalized symbols and to find instead solutions that more precisely suggest recent events.

The arrow symbols of the first group of solutions were tactical images and, therefore, more cerebral. The human form of the soldier, I felt, would better capture the reader's emotional attention. And because the figure was solitary, the soldier was more a human being than a member of any particular army.

On the basis of this reasoning, I traced the two-color sketch with the help of templates (9) and executed the finished art.

1

2

3

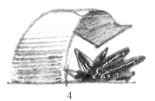

4

5

6

7

8

9

WAR IN LEBANON

MIDDLE EAST TIME BOMB

April 26, 1982

THIS SYMBOL linking stories on Middle East conflicts appeared in international editions of *Time* with extended coverage of problems in Lebanon and in the Sinai.

The idea was a simple one that actually might have been used to describe any of several potentially explosive situations in recent years: that of a time bomb whose fuse has already been lit. In this case, the symbol called for little development other than a carefully worked-out drawing, using templates to position the various elements involved (1). From this, I constructed art for reproduction, with a graduated tone-pattern to suggest the roundness of the bomb.

The final version ran in black with only a touch of red at the tip of the lighted fuse.

LEBANON BURNS

August 23, 1982

WHEN ANOTHER symbol was needed to describe the conflicts in Lebanon, we might well have used the one designed for an earlier issue (see page 61), which reported the siege of Beirut. That image was not specifically tied to any one city, and in retrospect, it might easily have been used as *the* Middle East war symbol.

Beirut hadn't been easily indicated in a symbol, but now, the nation of Lebanon could be. Moreover, some of the rejected sketches for the earlier solution lent imagery for this later one: a cedar of Lebanon, adapted from the country's flag, on fire.

The image was successful on many levels. The cedar was an image that by now had become visual currency in talking about the war in Lebanon. The blazing tree was also both figurative and literal in its imagery: trees can and do burn. And the color choices—green and brown for the tree (as on the flag) and red for the flame—provided a visual tension not unlike the tension inherent in the events themselves.

1

THE WOUNDED DOVE

April 25, 1983

THE PALESTINE Liberation Organization had walked away from talks with Jordan's King Hussein and had thwarted President Reagan's peace plan; the symbol used to connect the stories reporting these events was obvious: a peace dove wounded in flight.

Producing the symbol took little development: I simply placed a red drop of blood against the breast of a Matisse-like cutout of a dove. In the final version, a white highlight in the drop of blood lends dimension to an otherwise flat image.

ISRAEL'S BLITZ

June 21, 1982

IT MIGHT BE SAID that this was a symbol in search of a story.

For some time, I had had an idea for a symbol combining an arrow with the Star of David, and it was only a matter of waiting until the right opportunity came along to use it. Israel's tanks rolling into Beirut provided the chance I had been looking for.

By filling in certain parts of a six-pointed star, the star became an arrowhead (1). All that was needed to complete the idea was the addition of the arrow shaft to indicate movement and direction.

Although the symbol worked well in the context of the situation, in retrospect it seems more ambiguous. While some symbols can stand for all time, others work only in the limited circumstances for which they are created. This symbol is one of the latter.

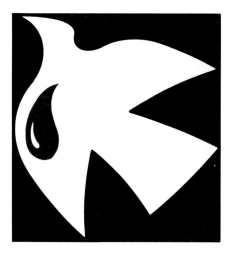

1

ANDROPOV: Three Symbols

February 20, 1984

FOR SOME TIME, the magazine had been planning a series of stories on Soviet leader Yuri Andropov, who had been in office one year at the end of 1983. But, as the Russian premier's health deteriorated, the stories kept changing, causing new symbols to be designed.

The first sketches for the subject were executed while Andropov was still healthy and active in office. As a straightforward exercise, these designs expressed his roles both as a military leader and as a politician (1). In each of these, the symbol idea was a matter of "looking through" one part of the man and the story into another—in visual terms, looking through a star shape to see a hammer and sickle. From one tracing (2), I prepared two versions in which only the placement of colors changed (3–4). But the idea never went to finished art; Andropov fell ill, and the story was shelved.

When word of his condition reached the West, *Time* editors began preparing Andropov's obituary, and I began thinking of a way to symbolize the fallen red warrior. The series of sketches (5) included versions of a red star robed in the black of mourning; a star lying prone, as if lying in state; a black star rising, Phoenix-like, and changing into a red one (to indicate the succession that would ultimately follow Andropov's death); a negative star shape, through which one could look to the future; and a red star poised at the rim of the earth, like a rising or setting sun.

This final image struck a responsive chord. Like the Phoenix concept, it carried with it the idea of succession, but here the concept was more immediately played out: the end of one day is always followed by the beginning of another. In the final drawing, the black sky was graduated, leaving Russia—and us—with some hope (6–7).

But again, this symbol wasn't used. Andropov hung on, and while the world speculated, Kremlin spokespersons were predicting an imminent recovery. When the end finally came, we reassessed the symbol I had designed. If Andropov had died when it first had been created, no doubt we would have used it. But now the editor was having second thoughts and asked me to try again.

At this point, I jotted down a series of images associated with death and the Soviets (8), including one of a Russian flag at half-mast. This design clearly conveyed the idea of the death of a Soviet public figure, and I tried three more versions (9), varying the square shape of the outline, which wasn't quite deep enough. By the final drawing (10), the square had become a rectangle, with the flag placed obviously below the halfway line.

It is interesting to note that this symbol uses the official Soviet flag, which positions the hammer and sickle in the upper left-hand corner, with a star above it.

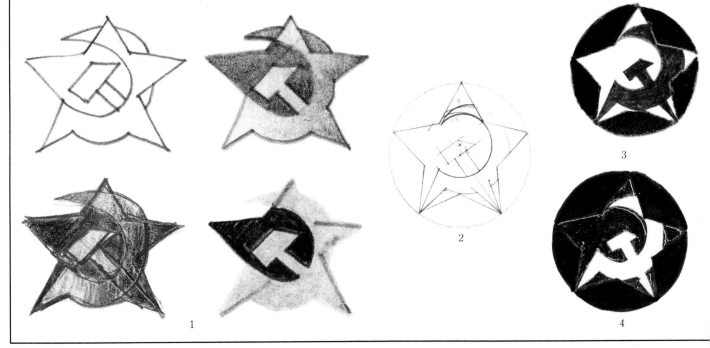

1

2

3

4

through to
the future

Rising / Setting star

5

6

7

Blue

8

9

10

IN THE AFTERMATH of the gunning down of a Korean Air Lines Boeing 747 jetliner over the Sea of Japan, *Time* published a group of stories probing the why and how of the Russian attack.

My first idea for a symbol to connect these reports and interviews was a play on the familiar Russian hammer and sickle—a bold red sickle cutting the airplane out of the sky (1). The jet itself was adapted from a drawing in one of the reference volumes I keep at my fingertips, *Jane's All the World's Aircraft*.

While I liked this idea, I sketched two others (2–3) to see how they would look. The first depicted a jetliner plunging within a red star; the second—a more emotional response—suggested a rush of murderous blood bringing the plane down from the sky. While both were possible solutions, neither had the visual twist inherent in the hammer-and-sickle design, which was the one we ultimately published (4).

1

2

3

4

SQUEEZING THE SOVIETS

January 28, 1980

TO DEPICT A series of stories about the Russian move on Afghanistan, an oversize, trodding paw of a large Russian bear might have been just the ticket (1). But the situation was more complex than that, and world reaction to the Russian incursion was editorially more important than the fact of the invasion.

By the time I came to do the symbol, the cover design by artist Doug Johnson had already been approved: a bear's forepaw caught in a bear trap as it stepped into Afghanistan (2). Designing the symbol, therefore, became a matter of reinterpreting the cover in a graphic sense.

The bear's paw was reduced to a basic shape with five thick, sharp claws extending from one end; the trap became a heavy diagonal line that was interrupted in the center by the paw. As its jagged, teeth-like edges "squeezed" the paw, the line seemed to be trying to reconnect itself, as if to form the international symbol for "Prohibited," which is indicated by a solid diagonal line.

The final drawing (3) prepared the way for the finished art, which transformed Johnson's stylish cover into a flat graphic symbol.

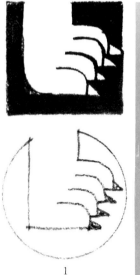

1

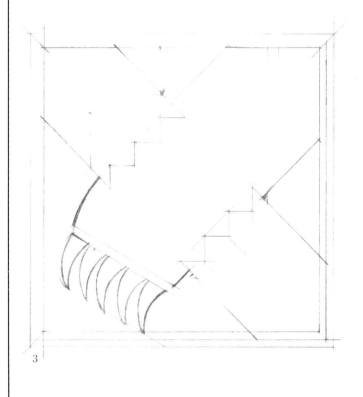

2

3

WORLD RECESSION
July 19, 1982

THE ARROW IS an ever-popular economic indicator, and it figured prominently in this symbol, devised for a group of stories on global recession: the result was a globe rolling down a bright red arrow.

This was a solution which presented itself straightaway. A quick pencil sketch (1) verified its viability; in redrawing it in color with tiny "motion" lines behind the globe (2), I saw that the arrow needed to be more dynamic and the earth set at a more precise tangent (3).

In the final sketch, I drew a thick red arrow on which to roll the globe, but the proportions were wrong, especially if the arrow were to be taken as an economic indicator. So I pared back the arrow by blocking it out with white tape (4), and the idea was ready for execution as repro art (5).

Somehow, unlike symbols that offer no clue as to their subject matter, this one works in or out of context, making a statement about some wordly affairs. And going downhill is something economies, in particular, do.

1

4

2

3

5

AMERICA AND RUSSIA
January 22, 1979; April 4, 1983

 IT HAS BEEN SAID that some symbols are successful only in the limited circumstances for which they are created, while others have a clarity and meaning that endures. One in the latter category is a symbol first developed in the days when *Time* ran only two colors in much of the magazine, and it depicted American–Russian relations.

At that time, the two superpowers had embarked on a policy that mixed confrontation with cooperation; to symbolize this policy, the simplest solution was also the most effective. Used first as an illustration (1), the red-and-black image consisted of two flags, the American and the Russian, devised as meeting arrows. The solution's ambiguity was apt: the arrows could be seen in confrontation, or as meeting at a common point. In the same issue, on a four-color page, the symbol was printed in full color as a corner tag (2).

Four years later, the possibility that the two superpowers could be headed for what *Time* called "a new, and highly destabilizing, arms race" arose as a result of a proposal that some people labeled the "Star Wars" defense—President Reagan's suggestion that laser and particle-beam weapons be mounted in space to destroy enemy missiles.

Interestingly, I developed essentially the same solution to describe this potentially dramatic phase of American–Russian relations. What was different about the symbol was not the basic concept but certain details of execution that reveal my own stylistic development during those four years.

While the earlier symbol had been more literal and quite careful in its rendering, this new version took liberties with the flag designs. I made only one sketch (3), in which I reduced the arrows of the earlier version to two simple triangles. In each triangle, I placed a stylized version of one of the flags. For the U.S., I no longer felt the need to include all thirteen stripes or the entire star field; instead, I divided the blue star field (*sans* stars) and drew in a pleasing number of stripes to yield an arrowhead. Similarly, I dropped the star from the Russian flag, leaving only the yellow hammer and sickle on a red ground.

The arrowhead flags were placed inside a square containing a graduated screen pattern. The pattern served to suggest the meeting of the two powers in space and also emphasized the arrowheads' point of contact.

GRENADA AND BEIRUT: Worth the Price
November 7, 1983

 BOTH A DRAMATIC rescue in Grenada and a brutal attack of a U.S. compound in Beirut involved Americans in emotional situations, and for successive stories on these events I proposed a set of three visually related symbols.

I planned to use an arrow-like symbol, formed from the U.S. flag, advancing on a tiny island for the Grenada piece (1); an exploding flag for Beirut (2); and, for a story on both, half of each symbol (3). I even went so far as to begin tracings of these ideas before I saw that they just weren't going to work.

Although I realized that the stories were actually two very different ones (with the U.S. being invited into Grenada and not wanted in Lebanon at all) and although I had worked very hard to make this first attempt communicate, my better judgment told me there was a need for separate symbols arising from the same visual language, so that the reader would see the stories as a related group.

The visual basis for the final solution came from the exploding-flag idea originally sketched for the Lebanon story (2). When I showed a new, tighter sketch of this concept to my colleagues, however, they thought it looked like an exploding boat (4). So I drew it again, with the explosion in a more fragmented, asymmetrical form (5).

My final sketch (6) shows a block-like object—the U.S. compound in Beirut—being blown up. In this sketch, I also tried to re-create the feeling of a large flag overshadowing a small island, as evoked in my first idea for Grenada. Ultimately, we used this fragmented-flag symbol with a small, triangular figure to signify an island for the Grenada report and with the block-like object for the report on Beirut (7–8).

Somehow, the sketches for these symbols seem more unified than the final art. There was a simplicity in the symmetry of the earlier versions which I prefer. But no explosion is symmetrical, and the final solution, in both literal and symbolic terms, is a better visual explanation than the sketches. Thus, my attempt to make two well-related symbols ended up not as I had planned.

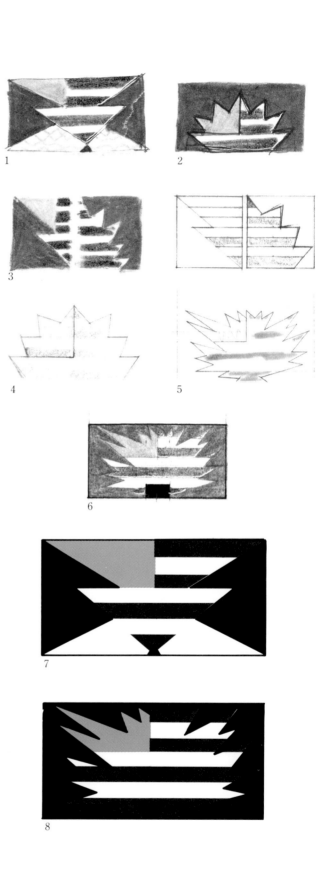

GRENADA AFTERMATH

November 14, 1983

THE CRISIS in Grenada had ended; the U.S. had pulled out, leaving a slightly uncertain situation behind. What would happen to this tiny island now?

Using the same colors as in the previous week's Grenada symbol, I experimented with the idea of a tropical island now at peace but with an uncertain red sky behind it (1–2), and the same island silhouetted against a blazing, sinking (or rising?) sun (3). One further attempt indicated a slight American presence by flying the U.S. colors from the silhouetted palm (4).

While these first sketches were executed with the island in close-up, my last sketch drew back, so that it seemed to float on an idyllic sea (5). Finally, I penciled in a red sky to leave some doubt in the reader's mind as to the state of affairs in this small piece of paradise.

This symbol ran with graduated tones of blue and red for the water and sky respectively (6).

1

2

3

4

5

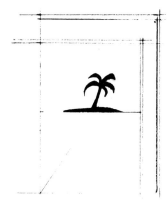

6

THE MX MISSILE
December 6, 1982

IT WAS THANKSGIVING weekend. We were visiting friends in Chicago when President Reagan made public his proposal of a new and controversial plan to deploy one hundred huge MX missiles in a cluster near Cheyenne, Wyoming; not long after the announcement, I received a telephone call from my editor back in New York. Would I design a symbol to link a last-minute group of stories about the MX?

After we hung up, I made a few scribbles and then dialed my assistant, Nino Telak. I told him we were about to design a symbol over the telephone, the idea being to create an "M" form that would both stand for "MX" and indicate the shape of the prodigious warheads.

Still on the telephone, I told him to draw a square. Then I told him to begin at the bottom left-hand corner and draw a line up to one-fourth the distance across the top of the square, back down to halfway across the bottom, up to three-fourths across the top, and finally back to the bottom right corner. He followed my directions, and now each of us had before him a large "M" shape within a square.

Next came the difficult task of accurately describing what I saw as highlights on the shiny surface of the "M." But having worked with me for a long time, Nino quickly grasped my meaning and interpreted the symbol correctly.

The cone-like shapes were printed solid black—the color of the warheads; the background was printed the bright yellow associated with nuclear energy and air-raid shelter signs.

PERIL IN CENTRAL AMERICA
March 22, 1982

 THE AGONIES of several Central American countries and a bungled attempt by the U.S. to document foreign subversion in El Salvador were the focus for this symbol, which was plainly inspired by the so-called domino theory that gained popularity during the Viet Nam War. Once again, nations were falling to Soviet interventionism, and the specter of a creeping Communism seemed very real.

I sketched two versions of this idea (1–2). In the first, a domino is seen in mid-flight, with its base poised above its shadow. In the second, the base is firmly rooted in the shadow. I chose the latter because of its greater feeling of stability and because it seemed to be falling backward much as a real domino would.

In the final art (3), which ran in black only, the shadow was laid in with a press-on pattern of graduated dots.

1

2

3

WAR IN NICARAGUA
October 17, 1983

IN THE MIDST of signs and banners painted with revolutionary rhetoric, the leftist Sandinista government in Nicaragua appeared to be girding for war with U.S.-backed counterrevolutionaries. For a series of stories discussing the political and social repercussions of the continuing strife in Nicaragua, the symbol neatly designed itself: a rifle superimposed on the Sandinista flag.

Flags always offer a designer a number of possibilities for symbol design because of their ready associations. Their colors and designs, which serve to identify a particular country or political entity, can be recognized in many configurations, leaving the flag's shape to become something else—a map, an arrow, an explosive outline.

In this case, the flag was used in a straightforward manner, as if unfurling from a staff, and since the design of the symbol called for little development, only one color sketch was made (1). From a second drawing, made by tracing over the sketch with templates (2), repro art was prepared.

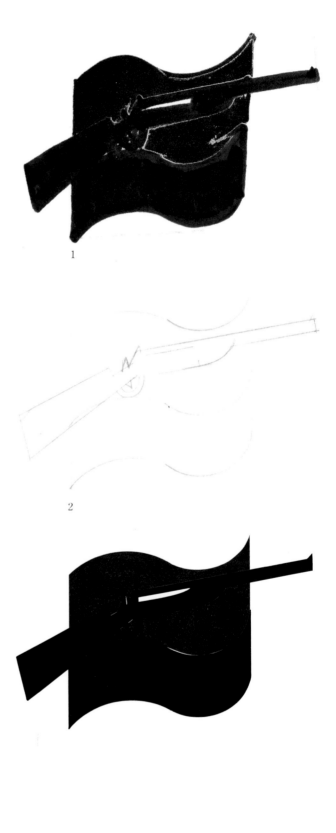

1

2

CENTRAL AMERICAN TROUBLES
March 14, 1983

 To connect a number of stories about politics and armed conflicts in various parts of Central America, we needed a symbol that was both general and specific. Because many countries were involved, no one flag could be used, and since the conflicts were guerilla wars, war images were not correct. There were also some questions posed as to whose side the U.S. should be on, who should receive U.S. financial assistance, and whether the U.S. should take sides or give money at all. Thus, the complexity of the situation demanded careful analysis before a symbol could be drawn.

The best solution, it seemed, would be to isolate this part of the world on a map (1). To do so, I employed cross hairs with a central red circle around the area involved. Outside the circle, there remained just enough of the map to allow the reader to identify the area in question. To heighten the effect, the land mass within the red circle ran in yellow with the circled ocean area in white; outside the circle, the land mass was black and the ocean was blue. On three-color pages, the blue became a gray tint.

The success of this symbol, which has seen repeated use in subsequent issues dealing with Central America, demonstrates the fact that many liberties can be taken with a map to simplify and stylize it before it begins to lose identity.

1

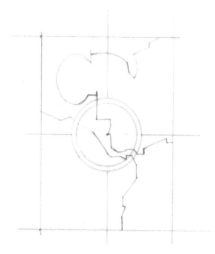

ELECTIONS IN EL SALVADOR
April 9, 1984

FOR A GROUP of stories about the controversial elections in El Salvador, I wanted to design a symbol that reflected what people had been saying all week— that the elections, in which voters braved threats and sometimes bullets to go to the polls, were a matter of "voting under the gun."

My first sketches experimented with this dual idea in a literal way (1): the "X" used to mark a ballot was made from crossed rifles and dropped into a ballot box. In this series, I also sketched the Salvadoran practice of fingerprinting each voter, but this idea was too obtuse for use as a symbol.

Returning to the central theme, I wrote out the phrase "voting under the gun" to fix it firmly in my mind. Still working with the ballot mark, I sketched several ideas—one placed the "X" before the cross hairs of a rifle, and one showed a marked ballot being dropped into the barrel of a gun (2). But while either of these ideas might have been acceptable to the editors, I wasn't happy with them.

I liked the "X" because it provided a natural incorporation of firearms and also suggested the "X" used as a signature mark. But it might also have been read as crossing something out, and the point of an election is, after all, to show approval. It seemed that a check mark might be more appropriate, and I included a series of sketches to test this idea (2).

At this point, I felt I had two viable alternatives, and I sketched them both at a larger scale for comparison (3). Of these, the check mark, it seemed, would most clearly represent the situation, provided that the rifle-shape could fit neatly within the check. Two more sketches, one rough and one more refined (4–5), resolved any doubts. From a tracing of the tighter drawing (6), I went on to prepare the finished art.

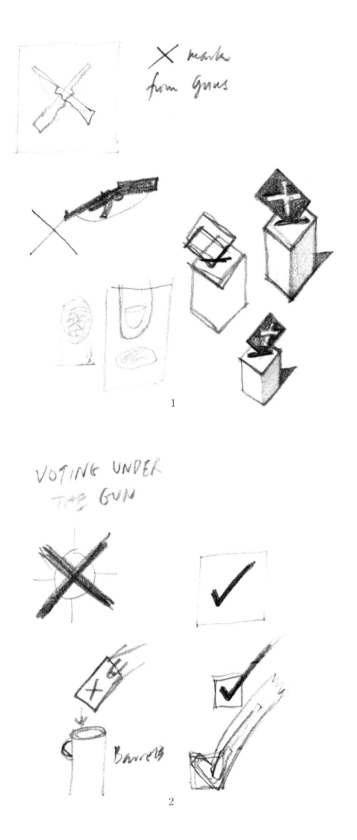

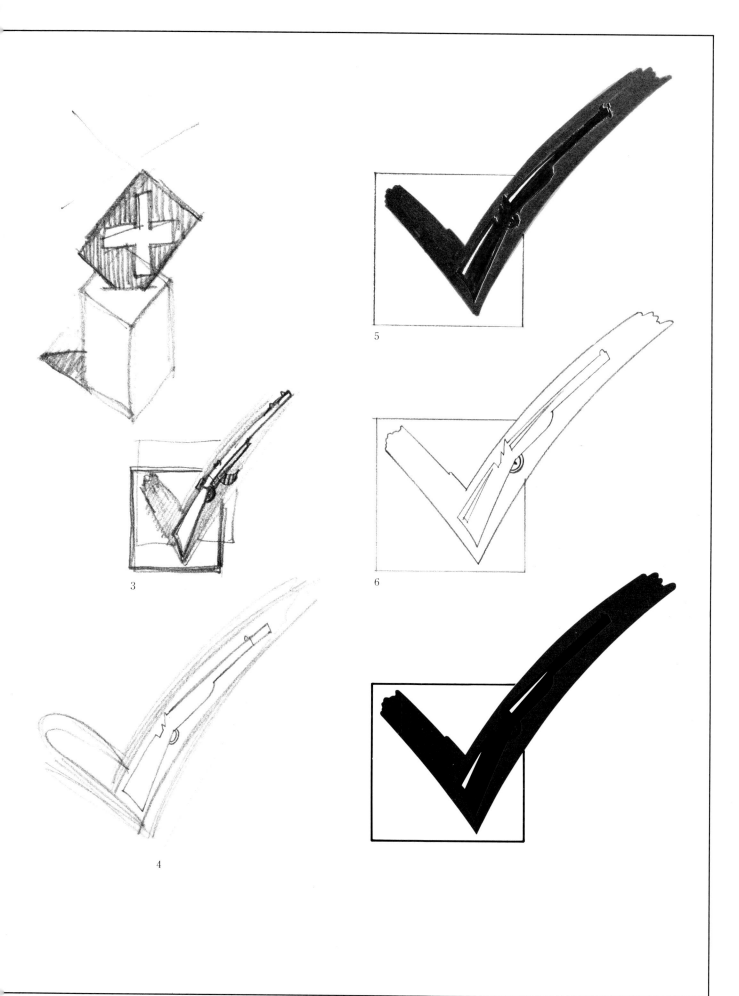

3

4

5

6

MINING NICARAGUA'S HARBORS

April 23, 1984

THE MINING of Nicaragua's harbors—and the subsequent revelations that the American CIA was involved in that mining—touched off an explosion of protest in the U.S. Congress and around the world. A clever cover-painting by David Suter summed up the situation: a floating White House was about to hit a marine mine whose detonators were formed from miniature Capitol domes (1).

Developing a symbol reflecting Suter's art was only a matter of a few hours. Indeed, my first idea was a literal adaptation of the Capitol-spiked mine (2). However, the building was really too complex to be reduced to symbol scale; and, besides, the mines—which we were showing in a diagram—really didn't look like that.

My next idea was a circular element floating in water. Adding spiky projections to the floating ball suggested an explosion; the blue water, which filled the lower half of the symbol square, was topped with tiny wavelets (2). I made several variations of this idea before presenting it to the editor, who was quick to okay it.

But when it came to final execution of the design, the waves got in the way of the spikes on the circle. It was also easier and faster to draw a straight line across the square to indicate the water's surface, and since time was important here, I took the simplest route (3).

1

2

3

CAMPAIGN 1980
January–November, 1980

AT THE BEGINNING of any general election year, thoughts begin turning toward the November polls, and news magazines begin coverage of the politicos-most-likely. The year 1980 was no different.

Since American political parties already have established symbols in the Republican elephant and Democratic donkey, there was no reason not to use them in talking about the 1980 Presidential campaigns. The trick was to make these symbols seem both fresh and relevant.

The first sketch (1) combined both images into a single symbol, the idea being to use color to distinguish which campaign was being discussed in any given article. This concept was especially appealing because it suggested the reliance of the parties on one another to make the U.S. two-party system work; unfortunately, the symbol wasn't as satisfying as the idea. So I went back to a more

1

2

conventional variation of the party symbols.

After a quick attempt at sketching full animal figures, it occurred to me that in the U.S. there was also a well-known visual symbol for political campaigns—the boater. Why not use it as well?

(It's interesting to note that in England the boater has an entirely different meaning, being associated with the Henley rowing regatta. Also, for an Englishman, it was nice to be working with real party symbols. In Great Britain, the parties are keyed only by color—red for Labour, blue for Conservative.)

A few sketches of the animals' heads, with and without the hats (3–5), served to establish a presentation style (clean and cartoon-like) and format (vertical). The extension of the donkey's ears and the elephant's trunk beyond the symbol frame added a bit of vitality and also helped define the symbol's shape on the page.

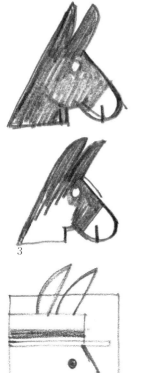

3

4

5

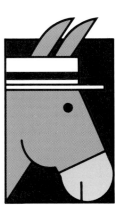

CAMPAIGN 1984

January–November, 1984

THE SYMBOL FOR the 1984 Presidential-election campaign started as a button designed by a freelance illustrator. After it ran in two issues, however, we felt that the design simply did not read clearly enough in such small scale. A decision was made to stop it before it had been used too often and we found ourselves locked into it. But what to use instead?

At first it seemed that with some cosmetic surgery, the original design might be made to work. It did not, but the idea of one image with lettering that could be changed as we rolled from primary campaigns through conventions to the elections themselves was good; so I continued in that vein for the new version.

The first attempts in this direction (1–3) were variations using block letters and the numerals "84," and the last of these was taken to full production (4–5) to see how well it would work. Type was set in Franklin Gothic—not hand-lettered, as in the original button—and the artwork was reduced to repro size. But I wasn't completely at ease with the solution.

In preparing a number of charts pertaining to the coming elections, I had already been using the donkey and elephant "dingbats" (6) available from *Time*'s in-house Atex typesetting facilities. It seemed that perhaps these should also be used somehow in the symbol itself, possibly with the elliptical areas in the numeral "8." At the same time, the whole "campaign button" concept was reconsidered. A square shape, with the appropriate word at the top, might be more easily read, and I prepared a sketch for that idea (7).

The sketch worked. After refining the idea (8) and experimenting with color (9), I settled on a blue field with a red strip at the top to hold the changing label. Both the label and the large "84" printed black, with the appropriate dingbat (the donkey or the elephant, depending on the story) dropped out of the "8" to paper white (10).

Interestingly, this symbol found another quite uncalculated use: a woman at the Democratic convention in San Francisco had clipped it from the pages of *Time* and had glued it prominently to her face!

6

7

8

9

10

PICTURING THE PRESIDENT
June 7, 1982; December 13, 1982

SOMETIMES IN the development of a pictorial symbol, one good image leads to another. Such was the case with the symbols for two groups of stories about President Reagan.

The first group of Reagan stories concerned the President's historic journey to Europe; in the same week, however, the Falklands crisis had reached its height; and the Pope had visited Britain, As a result, for only the second time in its history, *Time* magazine appeared with three unrelated cover subjects.

To connect the stories about Reagan's journey, it seemed that the simplest and most direct solution would be best. The idea of travel maps was rejected out of hand as too complicated, but there was another possibility—to somehow combine Reagan with a suitcase.

Using some campaign photographs as reference (1), I developed a Presidential silhouette with an exaggerated pompadour (2) so there could be no mistaking his identity. I then combined the silhouette with a suitcase in various configurations (3), as well as with an airplane and an arrow. The editors agreed that the sketch with the pompadoured silhouette inside a suitcase was the most direct, and this simple solution (4) appeared in a different color with each story.

2

3

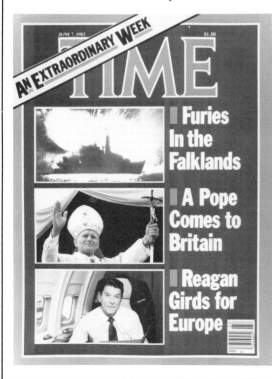

AN EXTRAORDINARY WEEK

JUNE 7, 1982 $1.50

TIME

Furies In the Falklands

A Pope Comes to Britain

Reagan Girds for Europe

4

Some six months later, with the President well established in his administration, *Time* ran a special report on his Presidency under the coverline "How Reagan Decides." Here, however, the solution was not at first so obvious; it was unclear whether the man or the office should be the focus of the symbol.

Initial efforts included placing the previously designed silhouette inside a dropped-out star, or using the star-shape as a window through which one could observe the White House (1). A second series of ideas included two variations on the Presidential seal (2). But after further consideration, it seemed that the crux of the stories was not the office but the officeholder—an evaluation of Reagan on the job.

The idea of evaluating—or "graphing"—Reagan was visualized by simply layering a press-on grid over the previously used silhouette (3). Because this idea related strongly to Mark English's cover portrait, which also used a graph-paper effect, it seemed like a winner. But a simple photostat of the sketch revealed that the whisper-thin graph lines were likely to be lost in reproduction.

The final solution, then, came down to the Presidential silhouette alone: it was both simple and apt (4). The original drawing was modified somewhat to curtail the pompadour: after nearly a year in office, the hair style itself had been the cause of much comment, and Reagan's profile was already well-known. The symbol was one of very few to run in black alone in all of *Time*'s editions.

BUILDINGS AS SYMBOLS
April 26, 1982; October 24, 1983

IN CERTAIN situations, a well-known building can be a perfect symbol for the activity that goes on inside it. Two cases in point are the U.S. Capitol and the White House, which can be read as Congress and the Presidency, respectively.

The U.S. Capitol building came into play for an issue of *Time* containing stories about various budget struggles going on within Congress. There was little time to develop a more abstract symbol, so I went right to the building itself; for this reason, I feel the symbol is probably one of the least successful ones I've done. It is straight-on and symmetrical, with no real opinion or style, although it does the job of alerting the reader.

In a series of sketches where I tried to play with form and abstraction, I used color to shape the building (1), but the symbol obviously needed the added definition of a drawing (2). The final sketch and tracing (3) quickly became finished art (4).

The White House symbol, for a later issue containing a number of political stories about the Presidency, was similarly a pictorial rather than symbolic solution; the problems in its development had more to do with the shape of the building itself than with the obviousness of the solution.

With its front colonnade and side wings, the White House assumes a long, thin shape not well-suited to the square symbol-space that we typically use in the magazine. To solve this problem, the building was cropped on the sides and placed in an oval that would suggest both a cameo and the shape of the President's office, as well as "fatten" the shape.

Only one sketch of the building was made, in full color (5), then quickly taken through tracing to finished art (6–7).

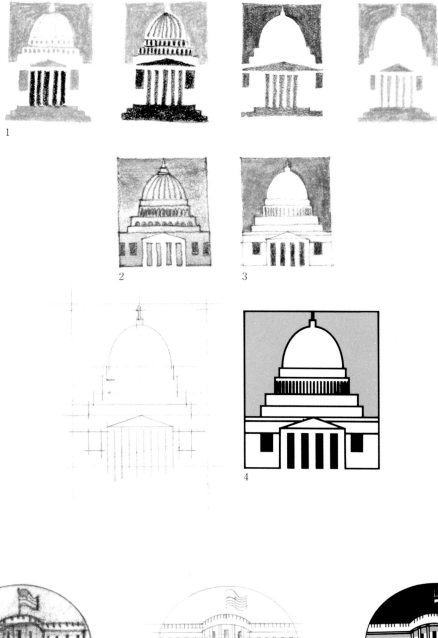

2

1

THE GRAIN HARVEST AS A WEAPON
January 21, 1980

TO SYMBOLIZE a series of stories arising from the politically motivated embargo of U.S. grain exports to Russia, I decided that a simple image of a stalk of wheat would be the most direct solution. And yet, this symbol took no little effort to develop into a usable form.

The difficulties stemmed from the wispy fibers surrounding each ear: the question was how to reproduce them in such a small scale. Leaving them off reduced the ear to a cluster of berries; rendering them in their natural proportion made them illegible. Hence, the first attempts at symbolism here focused on developing what seemed a more manageable image—a whole sheaf of wheat (1). But the sheaf, it turned out, was even more complicated, and I went on to develop something usable with a single ear.

The next series of sketches tackled head-on the problem of the wisps. After finding a shape I liked (2), I worked at subtle refinements by bending the wisps, adding and deleting space between the kernels, and reducing the size of the grains (3). I discovered that with no space around the kernels, the image did not read well; with a bit of space added between each kernel and the stem, the image did not occupy its circular frame well. When I tested this last concept as a drop-out (as I envisioned the final art), I found that while these little spaces were not filling in, the wisps were all but disappearing (4).

In developing new art (5), I corrected the problem by making the wisps slightly bolder and opening them at a different tangent from the grains. This shape occupied a more pleasing part of the symbol circle and held its own when reversed and reduced. Reproduction was in a fresh green.

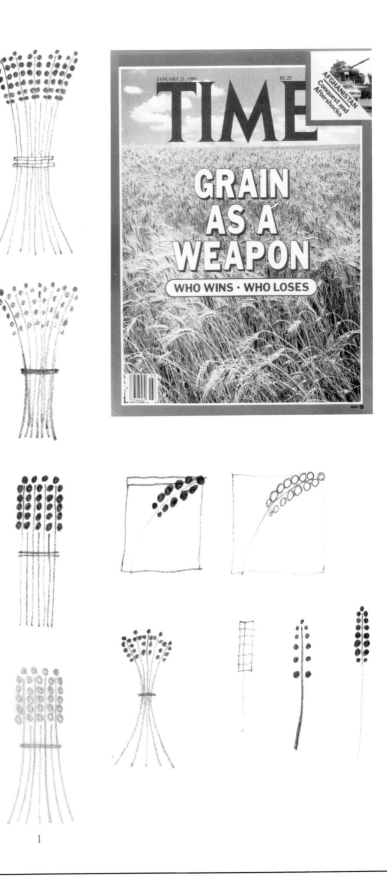

1

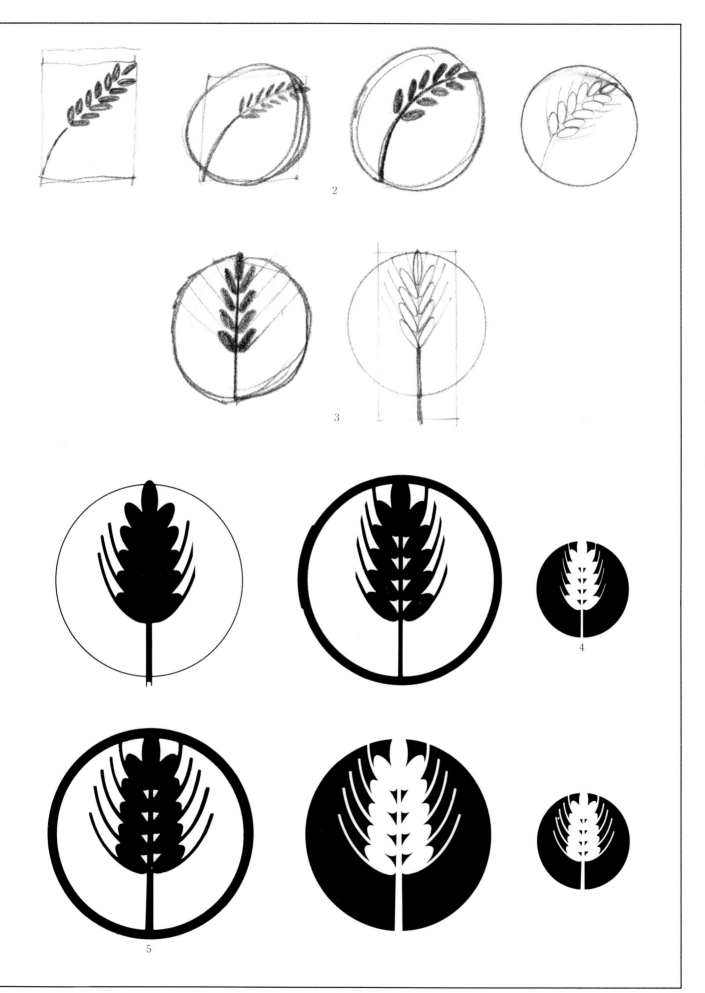

2

3

4

5

IMMIGRATION
February 22, 1982

A SYMBOL to connect a series of articles on immigration patterns both in the U.S. and around the world provides an object lesson in how to simplify a well-known object. And what could be a more likely symbol for immigration than the one that has stood in New York Harbor for nearly one hundred years?

The first step was tracing the Statue of Liberty from a high-contrast photo in which the statue was strongly lit from one side. Then I filled in the darker areas of the statue, leaving just enough white highlights at the left to give the form definition (1). To have turned the figure into a single-toned silhouette simply wouldn't have worked, as much of the statue's identity would have been lost.

This drawing was statted down to around four times the repro size (2), then traced and filled in with black ink for reproduction. Dating from the period before *Time* had four-color capability on every page, the symbol was run in solid black.

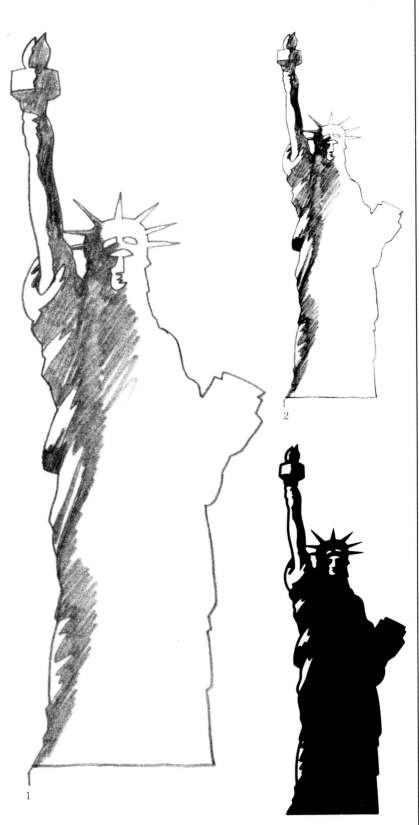

1

2

THE NEW BABY BLOOM

February 22, 1982

THIS SYMBOL taught me the meaning of the minimal mark, and my lesson began with a simple circle and a pair of shoe-button eyes.

There was no question but that the symbol for the new baby "bloom" should be a baby's face, and that to become a baby's face, it needed to be round. Thus, finding the right solution became a matter of experimenting with facial features—the shape and placement of eyes, nose, and mouth—and deciding whether or not the baby should wear a lock of hair curled against its forehead (1).

I quickly discovered that the tiniest change in the size or placement of any of these elements drastically altered my feelings about the baby in question. When I came to refining my initial attempts, I found that two dots for the eyes—the absolute minimum to say "face"—made the symbol into a button, so I added the curl (2). It was still too minimalist, so I added full features for the final drawing (3)—a perfectly lovable face, not quite symmetrical and slightly quizzical in aspect.

And, of course, I colored it pink.

Expectant Actress
Jaclyn Smith

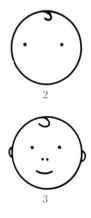

2

3

1

THE U.S. IN SPACE

November 26, 1984

IT WAS A TIME of high drama. The United States space program, which in recent months had suffered some setbacks, had scored a smashing success: the shuttle *Discovery* had salvaged two wayward satellites, proving, in the words of the title-page blurb, that NASA still had the right stuff. *Time* editors decided to make the event the cover story and to back it up with four other stories about man in space—one about the business of space technology, one assessing other countries' progress in space, one that would more closely examine U.S. progress, and one that would feature some of the recently published photographs made by astronaut–physicist Joseph P. Allen during a previous shuttle mission.

The photographs appearing with these stories were awe-inspiring and conveyed a real sense of the vastness of space. I wanted to capture this feeling in the symbol that was to link the stories, and several shots of the starry void seeming to stretch into infinity influenced my first thoughts.

The idea here was to create an amorphous starfield that would break our usual symbol conventions by extending into the margin and behind the text (1, 2). But then a layout decision made this symbol impractical: the "action" space shots were to be inset into larger shots of the starry field, and to juxtapose these with a starfield symbol would have been too chaotic. I tried confining the field to a square (3), but this only destroyed the infinite feeling I was trying to create.

To recapture some of the depth, I added a portion of the earth in the foreground (4, 5). This solution seemed far too ordinary to convey the excitement inherent in the event and its implications, and I began to look for another image. The idea of a rocket blasting off was attractive because I could use the accompanying burst of smoke to stretch the symbol frame, much as I had with the starfield concept (6, 7). However, these images were more descriptive of a moonshot than a shuttle mission and, in any event, too hardware oriented.

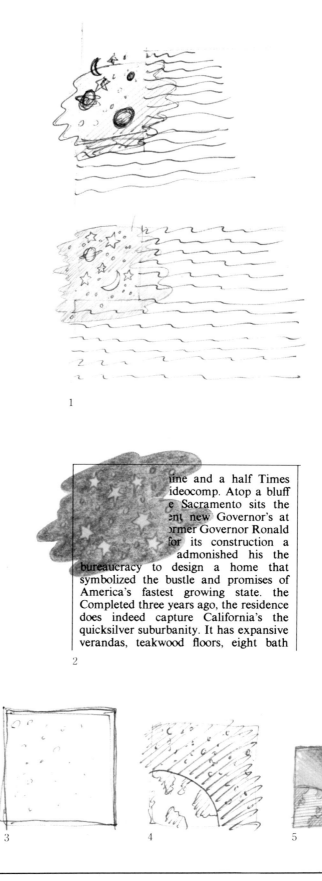

ine and a half Times ideocomp. Atop a bluff e Sacramento sits the ent new Governor's at ormer Governor Ronald for its construction a admonished his the bureaucracy to design a home that symbolized the bustle and promises of America's fastest growing state. the Completed three years ago, the residence does indeed capture California's the quicksilver suburbanity. It has expansive verandas, teakwood floors, eight bath

...ked a carter tide to vote for Hayakawa
Ford. Some argue that the peak came
his is ten on nine and a half Times
...an, set on the Time Inc. Atex Copy
...essing System. When gasoline the
...tages tarnished the freeways and
...bs anchoring California's life style.
...rs insist that the curtain fell last year,
when citizens realized the inevitability of
an earthquake and the consequences of a
drought. But everyone agrees that the
California of the a mystical land of
abaundance and affluence vanished some
time in the seventies. This is Ten on nine

6

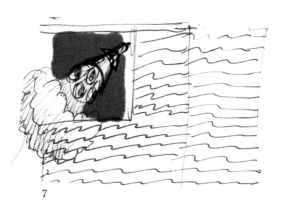

7

My second group of ideas were at first more abstract—an eye with a starry cosmos in the center, a telescope, and a space boot appended with the wings of Mercury (8–10). All attempted to express the idea of man looking forward to his future in space. Then a new kind of image occurred to me: a human figure, feet earth–bound, reaching for the stars (11). It seemed to say everything about America's hopes for her space program, and I tried several versions in color (12–15).

I instinctively liked this idea, but, given the limitations of the symbol's scale, it was difficult to design a figure with the right proportions—it was either too fat or too thin. When I reversed the image (14), it turned into a snowman in a snowstorm, and when I thinned it down too much (11, 13), it looked like a starving person reaching for help—a solution especially inappropriate for an issue that also contained a report on the famine in Ethiopia. I tried reducing the figure to a simple human hand (16), but this solution seemed to take on religious overtones.

I was at an impasse. I really wanted the man reaching for the stars to work (15), and given more time for development, I think it would have. However, with only a day to design a symbol, I was forced to choose one both appropriate and close to completion. In considering the options, the "ordinary" one seemed most likely (4): it combined both earth and space, and its square proportions didn't fight with the layout. I worked it up quickly in color to establish positioning (17, 19) and made a tracing (18) to prepare the final art (19).

a mystical land of
...luence vanished some
...s. This is Ten on nine
...oman set on the Atex
... and run through the
...den epoch that gave
...a dream began when
...ned over the loss of its
...ked west for spiritual
renewal. On the edge of the horizon it
found California. Heretofore dismissed
for its aimless spirit and shallow purposed,
California seemed reborn or at least
exciting. While think tanks scanned the

17

18

19

WAR IN THE FALKLANDS

THE BRITISH crisis in the Falkland Islands off the coast of Argentina was not a single event but an ongoing story demanding different symbols each week to represent specific events as the situation changed.

THE BRITISH MOVE SOUTHWARD
April 19, 1982

IN THE FIRST instance, a symbol was needed to introduce readers to these heretofore largely unknown isles—hence, an early solution comprised of a simple map (1) with the islands circled. Then, to put forth the idea of conflict, I sketched around the islands two opposing forces, as identified by their flags (2); the islands between two gun barrels (3); and two guns crossed in the South Atlantic (4).

At this point I was preparing some maps to accompany the report, and these were influencing my thinking, so that the shape of the islands seemed important. Further sketching produced both protecting and grabbing hands (5–8), and the islands themselves sitting in water with the Union Jack approaching (9)—although this last bit seemed more like an English expedition to find the Loch Ness monster. As the week drew to a close, there suddenly seemed no need to picture the little lumps of islands at all, and this last sketch began to look more hopeful.

I began to work up the idea once more, this time in color (10–11). The Union Jack, remodeled to include an arrow, strongly suggested Britain's navy moving south through a rippling sea. The water itself was developed from a press–on pattern, with the space between the lines filled in in graduated distances to suggest depth (12, 13).

In retrospect, this first symbol (14) could have been used fairly aptly throughout the Falklands confrontation. But since the U.S. played a key role as Britain's ally, the symbol was too one–sided. It was for the best that later symbols pictured other facets of the developing situation.

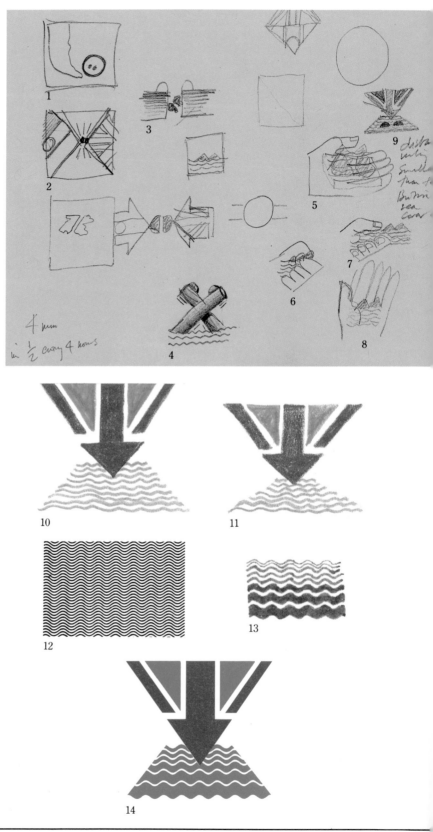

THE SINKING OF THE *BELGRANO*
May 17, 1982

DURING THE week covered by *Time*'s May 17 issue, the most important event was the sinking by the British of the Argentine cruiser *General Belgrano*. There was little development in symbolizing this event; sketches of an explosion and a sinking ship (15, 16) brought a quick solution. A tracing of the latter smoothly worked out the details (17); from there it was a simple step to finished art, which was executed with an original drawing and a press-on pattern of dots (18).

15

16

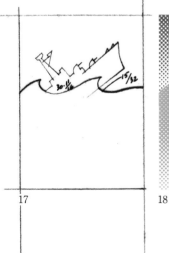

17

18

THE LANDING OF THE BRITISH
May 31, 1982

BY THE TIME preparations were being made for the May 31 issue, we were anticipating the arrival of the British fleet in the Falklands and a swift resolution of the situation there. The idea of arrival seemed key, and my initial sketches reflect this concept (19). Another group (20) deals more closely with the ships themselves, and of these, one seemed particularly promising.

The next group of sketches—now in color—made variations on that one: a British warship steaming head-on toward the landing—and the reader (21–24). The task here was to find the right configuration of guns, wake, and bow. Executed at three times repro scale, all of these sketches were too complex and ornate for the final solution. I selected the most likely (21) and did a fold-over tracing that produced a simplified and symmetrical drawing on which to base the finished art (25, 26).

19

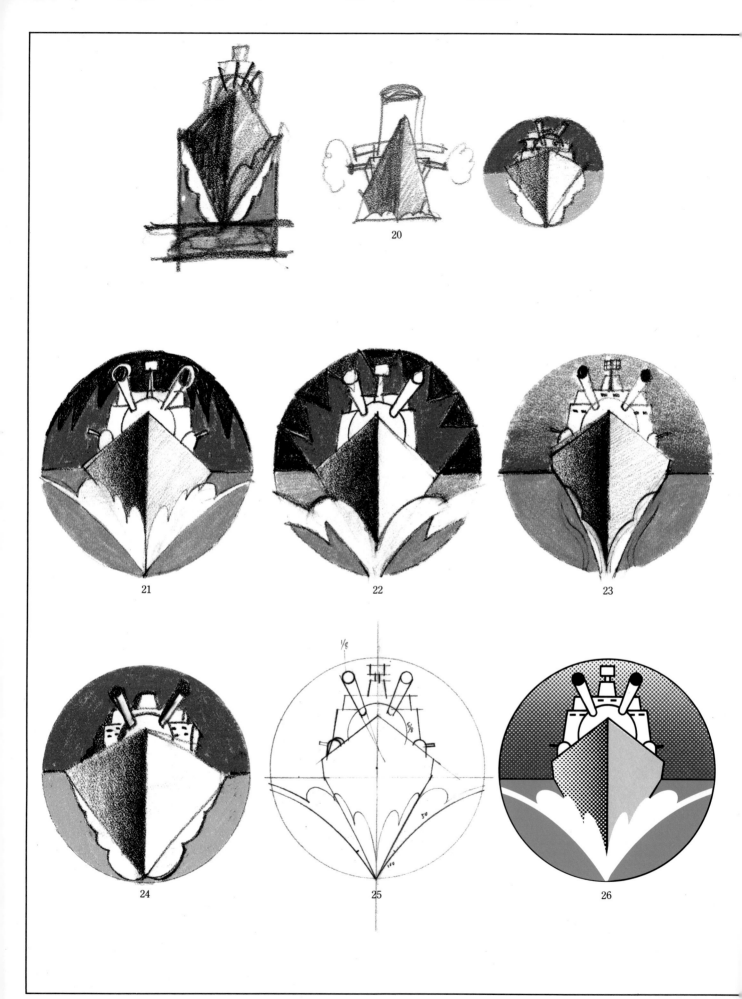

20

21

22

23

24

25

26

AN ATTACK ON ARGENTINA

June 7, 1982

 THE BATTLE for the Falklands had become a question of ownership and the islands themselves an ideological battleground. There was no question but that the Argentinians would be flushed out; it was more a matter of how long they would resist. The Argentine government had been misrepresenting the progress of the war to its citizenry for its own purposes, and as the world looked on, some political questions developed, albeit a little late in the game: Was this a just war? On whose side did America belong?

The subject for the symbol at this point became an attack on Argentina, and there was only one sketch made (27). The Union Jack-*cum*-arrow, used with the magazine's initial coverage, was called into play, this time advancing on a simplified version of the flag of Argentina. A simple tracing prepared the way for the finished art (28, 29).

THE FINAL SURRENDER

June 14, 1982

 THE LAST REPORT on the Falklands conflict was a story of surrender. This seemed the perfect opportunity to use the heraldic British lion, which to British political lore is equivalent to the American eagle. With its overlord image and trappings of sovereignty, it seemed to signify most aptly the reconfirmation of the Falklands as an outpost of the British Empire.

The first sketch—a pictorial rendering (30)— simply wasn't strong enough to convey the might of the British victory, and the second—more heraldic, with a snarling, victorious pose (31, 32) —was a considerable improvement.

FALKLANDS POSTSCRIPT:
Elections in Argentina

November 14, 1983

 ONCE AGAIN, a symbol was designed from a simple decision and a mental image brought swiftly to reality, and, once again, the image began as a flag.

Here, the sun from the Argentinian banner was adapted with all its shining rays intact; in the foreground, as if rolling away to reveal the shining shape, were placed simplified clouds whose puffy shapes were formalized into connecting arcs (33).

The decision to retain the complexity of the sunform in this instance was made in consideration of the clouds: the "fiddliness" of the rays provided the perfect foil to their smooth, rolling edges.

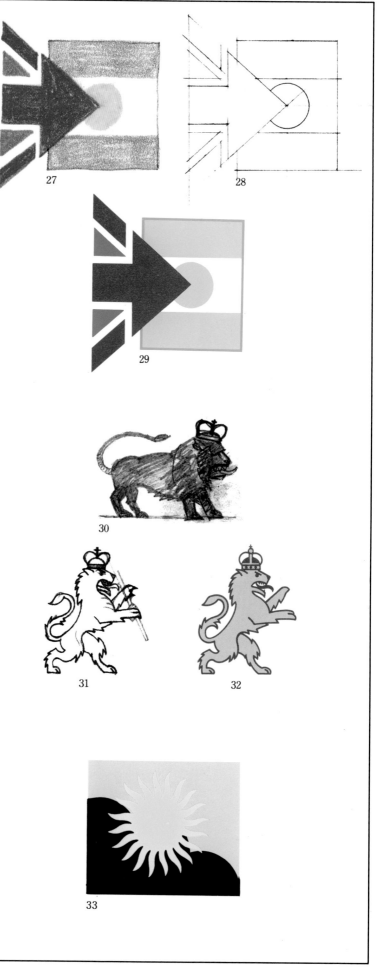

27

28

29

30

31

32

33

AMERICAN RENEWAL: Story of a Print Campaign

In a way, designing a symbol for Time Inc.'s special editorial project, "American Renewal," was not too different from the kinds of symbol assignments I tackle routinely at *Time* magazine. Like those, this problem called for one symbol, representing a common idea, to be used with a series of stories on the same topic. However, the American Renewal symbol had to be used with perhaps a dozen different articles, covering a broad range of viewpoints, in all of Time Inc.'s magazines.

The idea behind the project, which was originally entitled "American Revival," stemmed from a deep-felt concern on the part of the company's editors regarding what they perceived as the corrosion of the American Dream. A once confident and prosperous nation seemed to be bending under the weight of rampant inflation, a cumbersome and expensive government, and diminished industrial productivity. America had become, in the words of Time Inc. editor-in-chief Henry Grunwald, a democracy that "too often produces only mediocrity and deadlock." And if this was the situation at home, America abroad had suffered a loss of position in both trade and military credibility in a world that seemed increasingly hostile to her.

To instill hope and find the resilience and strength for recovery, Time Inc. initiated a month-long editorial project aimed at awakening all the best of what it is to be "American"—to start an "American Renewal." This revival, as Grunwald wrote in his introduction to the project which appeared in the February 23, 1981 issue of *Time* and all other Time Inc. magazines, "will not be accomplished by rhetoric, chest thumping, self-hypnosis. It will take great and disciplined effort and

exact a considerable price. It will also require a virtue rare in America: patience."

Through a number of different articles appearing in Time Inc.'s seven magazines—*Time, Life, Sports Illustrated, People, Money, Fortune,* and *Discover*—each magazine explored the theme as related to its own subject matter, each addressing a different set of issues and suggesting what might and should be done. In this way, Time Inc. hoped to spur its 68 million readers into the vanguard of a nationwide movement—a movement well beyond the realms of politics, economics, and defense, and encompassing "ethics, morale, social, and spiritual values."

There were articles on governmental reform and patriotism; industrial competition and productive business investment; inflation, energy, education, and discrimination. There were calls to individual responsibility; assessments of scientific progress on earth and in space; lessons in discipline and teamwork.

And all of these discussions had to be linked by one symbol that would make sense regardless of topic, from story to story, magazine to magazine.

My first meeting with the editors was brief. Essentially, I was in competition with two outside designers, who were also being asked to offer ideas and prepare sketches. The concepts the editors liked best would be developed further, until one designer—and one symbol—prevailed. The symbol was to be optimistic: although there were some things amiss in America, the editors intended to set them right. And although the stories that the symbol was to enhance had not yet been written, the editors knew they would be dealing with all facets of American life, from economics and the pursuit of excellence, to family, political power, and volunteerism.

PHASE ONE

Using the concept of "American Revival," my first ideas involved America's own great graphic symbol—its flag. I envisioned the flag as both an embodiment of American patriotism and as some kind of framework for all the good things that were part of American life. I tried to symbolize the latter in a series of rough sketches that incorporated a landscape, a mirror, a check mark, a rainbow, a room with a view, a view down a road, or "smiling" stripes (1). I hoped one of these would aptly convey to Americans a feeling about themselves—a reflection of America rolling up its sleeves and achieving a revival from within. But somehow, the combination of flag and picture seemed a bit cumbersome. I abandoned the flag and decided I only needed the ideas. The next step was to try to work the ideas into something else, within an eye-catching symbol form.

It turned out that my first experiments revolved around a part of the flag—a single star. This group of sketches (see following two pages) saw a sunrise within a star (2–4), a flag within a star (5, 6), and a star that was also an arrow (6–9). Still struck by the immediacy of the flag as a visual symbol, I also experimented with the idea of the flag itself becoming an upturned arrow (10, 11)—and at last I felt I was approaching a real solution. I made two more series of sketches exploring this idea (13–24).

By returning to earlier sketches, I found that certain of them suggested real movement—the smiling bars, for example. If the bars could move why couldn't they be going up? To enhance the element of motion I created a third dimension in the flag (13), adding a shadow that made the arrow seem to lift off (14, 15)—this time with the shadow in the shape of a map of America.

With the final group of sketches in Phase One (16–19), I returned to the straight-arrow concept (the flag as space ship) and also tried bending the flag into a rainbow and a smile (20–22). At this point I abandoned other attempts at visualizing an eagle and a multicolored Liberty crown (22, 24).

In reviewing these rough sketches, I selected those I felt held the most promise for meeting the complicated requirements of the task. Keeping in mind the various needs and limitations for color printing in the different magazines, I developed these black-and-white efforts into color roughs in Phase Two.

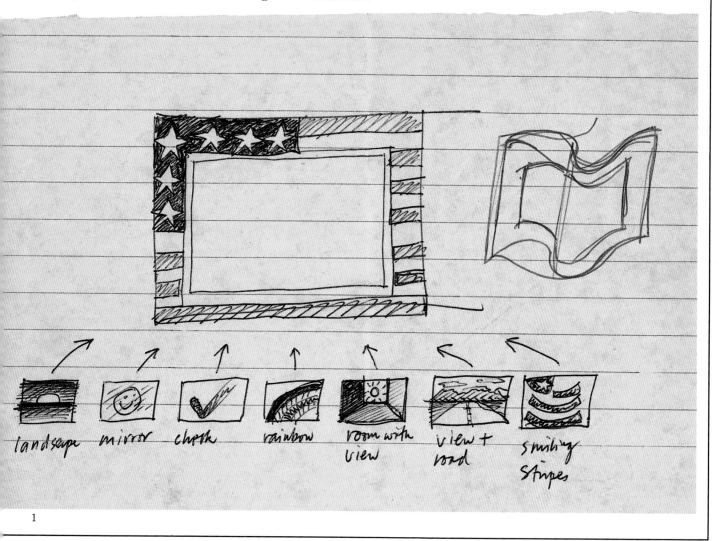

1

landscape   mirror   check   rainbow   room with view   view + road   smiling stripes

13

14

15

16

17

18

19

20

21

22

23 Blue R white

24

PHASE TWO

Applying color to the rough sketches executed in Phase One brought further definition to my ideas. By outlining a star shape in two or three colors, I was able to add new depth to the landscape inside it (25–28). Similarly, the star-arrow configuration, which had seemed rather bland in black and white, took on new life when executed in bright red and blue (29–31). At this time, I also made a variation on the flag-and-star that I had toyed with briefly in Phase One (32), and added color to several other designs (33–39).

The vertical arrow was instinctively quite interesting; it was quite direct. I even went so far as to start to figure out how the stars and stripes would fit (40, 41).

As a last-minute thought, I made some tight sketches utilizing three variations of the star symbol, along with the words "American Revival." (42–45) But upon presentation to the editors, the use of any words with the symbol was prohibited and, at the same time, the name of the project was changed to "American Renewal."

25

26

27

28

29

30

31

32

33

34

35

36

37

38

39

40

41

42

43

AMERICAN REVIVAL

44

45

PHASE THREE

By a discriminating review of the color sketches, I arrived at a limited number of designs to be tightly sketched for presentation to the editors. During this phase, I resolved certain details of execution—for example, the rendering of points or corners on the star design (46, 47)—in preparation for final artwork.

The ten designs I presented in this round included four groups that were variations on a theme—the star-and-landscape (48, 49), which were rendered with colored pencils and markers; the star with flag, arrow, or pyramid (50–53), in pencil, ink, marker, and Cellotak for large color areas; ink-and-marker renderings of the lifting ar-row, both with and without the shadow-map (54, 55); and two versions of the vertical "spacecraft" arrow (56, 57), also executed in ink and marker.

Of these designs, the editors liked the vertical arrows best; in the opinion of *Time* editor-in-chief Henry Grunwald, this concept said the most about the idea of American Renewal. The rainbow, which I had carried through in my rendering of the pyramid, they felt was a bit overused; the landscape-and-star seemed too decorative; while the star-and-arrow seemed too simple. They asked me to develop the idea of a flag rising as an arrow, and all other ideas—whether mine or my outside competitors'—were left behind.

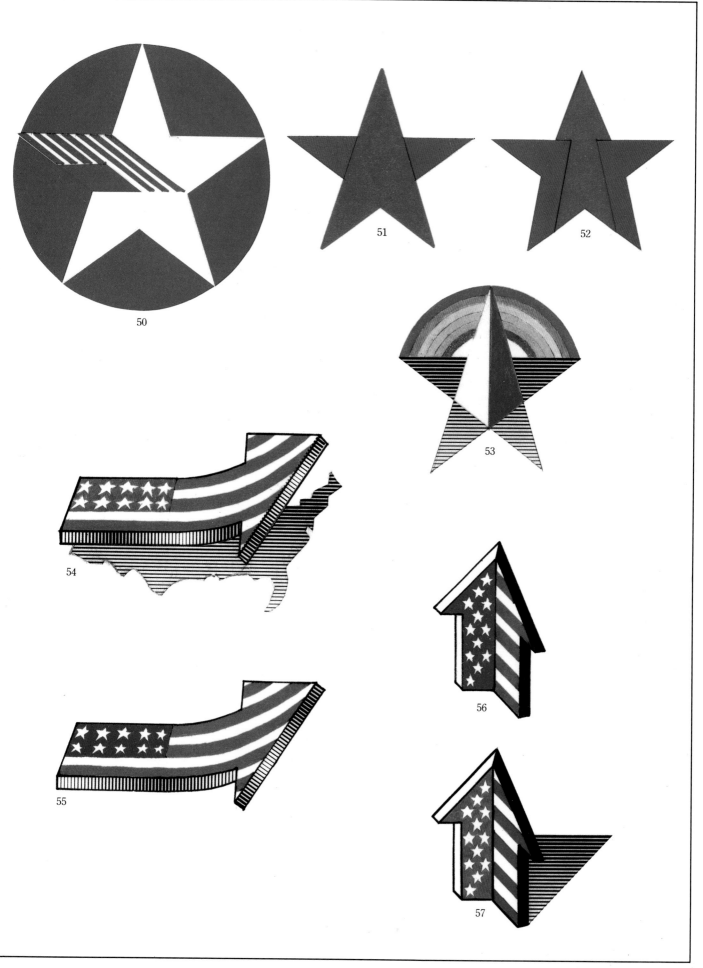

PHASE FOUR

The final leg of the American Renewal symbol project consisted of experimentation and refinement of the "rising arrow" symbol chosen by the editors at the close of Phase Three. This meant redrawing the symbol according to two basic approaches—a vertical arrow, and an angled one. I executed each of these concepts with stars and stripes variously left or right, above or below, the arrow axis (58–61).

Of this group, I and the editors all felt the angled star, which pointed right at 45 degrees, was the best solution. I flopped one of these, so that its stars were on the right and its stripes were parallel to its base (61). This *looked* good—but it meant the image of the flag was backwards. A discussion on propriety followed.

After weighing the concept and its purpose, the editors felt that the design as it stood was unobjectionable. It was not a matter of using a real flag, they reasoned, but of an arrow formed from flag elements. It seemed more important, for the sake of balance in the design, to execute the stripes running horizontally. Interestingly, at the time no one thought of putting the stripes to the right of the axis—a position which would have been natural on both accounts. In retrospect, I think this solution would probably not have worked anyway—the stripes at the top would have been unacceptably truncated by the point of the arrow. This flopped sketch (61) was ultimately approved for final execution and preparation for printing.

The final design (62) was executed using Cellotak, ink, and white Letraset stars, and several refinements from the approved sketch were made during the process. For one, the sketch showed only twelve stripes (six red, six white); the final, like the American flag, alternates red and white bars for a total of thirteen. Additionally, the placement of the stars needed to be carefully worked out, and this was accomplished, through trial and error, by groupings of three stars along both vertical and horizontal axes. The stars appear to be in parallel rows, but actually they are only vertically parallel. As the rows of stars step upward along the angle of the arrow, their horizontal points can be seen to shift upward, too, and slightly out of line—forming a cluster of stars that are optically "correct" while at the same time conforming to the limitations of the arrow shape.

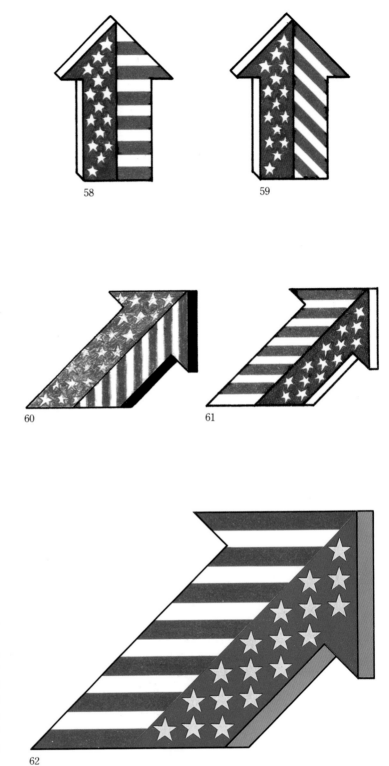

58

59

60

61

62

APPLICATIONS

Using the final artwork, I had C-prints made and sent them to the art directors of each magazine for use in designing their American Renewal layouts. In addition, the design was separated into Amberlith overlays for four-color reproduction as well as two-color applications. Ultimately, the symbol appeared within each magazine's own design vernacular, in domestic as well as international editions, without losing its power as a unifying element. The editors were so pleased with the solution that one of them quipped, "(This) arrow is the most famous arrow since William Tell's."

American Renewal

It is entirely possible, but it is not inevitable. It will take great effort and exact a considerable price. It will also require a rare virtue: patience. Self-interest rightly understood is what we must retrieve.

The belief in an ever-better tomorrow, the conviction that obstacles exist to be overcome and that the U.S. has a strong and beneficial role to play in the world—these constitute the American secular religion. For some time now, that religion has been corroded by doubt. Intractable inflation seems to have turned the good life into a treadmill and has shaken our confidence in the future—America's last frontier. Our industry appears to have lost its productive magic, its daring, and sometimes even its competence. Our government is intrusive, inept—and expensive. Our democracy too often produces only mediocrity and deadlock.

Abroad, allies whom we rescued from the shambles of World War II defy us, former enemies whom we defeated now often outproduce and outtrade us. Our power is challenged by growing Soviet ambitions and military prowess, by OPEC's endless extortions, by a chaotic, largely hostile Third World. Much of this situation was symbolized by two recent events that showed the U.S. relatively powerless: Russia's invasion of Afghanistan and the Iranian hostage crisis.

Is this what has become of the American Century?

Not really. America's domestic and foreign crises are genuine. But they have been widely exaggerated. The U.S. is more self-critical than any other nation; it is also more resilient than most. The U.S. has not suddenly turned into a second-rate power, or even (as is sometimes suggested) into just another big power. It remains unique. It has immense resources—physical, intellectual, spiritual—that are not being fully or rightly used. An American renewal is entirely possible. But it is not inevitable. It will not be accomplished by rhetoric, chest thumping, self-hypnosis. It will take great and disciplined effort and exact a considerable price. It will also require a virtue rare in America: patience.

That is the theme of the special editorial undertaking by all of Time Inc.'s magazines this month: American Renewal.

The need for renewal ranges well beyond economics, politics and defense; it encompasses ethics, morale, social and spiritual values. That fact and a desire to reach the largest possible audience are the reasons why we decided to spread this special project among all our publications, including those not primarily concerned with public policy. In more than a score of articles altogether, each of the magazines treats a different set of issues and offers suggestions about what should be done.

We have not tried to cover every topic worthy of attention, and we make no claims to unique answers or unique wisdom. We expect disagreement and debate. But as journalists who believe that our role should be constructive as well as critical, we have given the nation's problems much thought; we also have made a sizable effort to sift the thinking of others and to present what we believe to be the best and most promising proposals. We hope that concerned citizens and experts, in many groups, organizations, schools and colleges—possibly even in government—will consider these issues anew. Our chief purpose is to dispel the notion that nothing can be done. Thus we also report on many people who have in fact done a great deal, have already begun their own American Renewal.

Work on the project started last May, long before the outcome of the election was discernible. Some of our recommendations parallel Reagan Administration policies or promises; many differ sharply from them. In general, we have not worried about what seems politically easy or feasible but about what seems right.

America's ills are attributed to changes abroad and, variously, to lack of will, failure of nerve, moral decay, selfishness and sloth, the shattering of community feeling. One can find signs of all of these, but the key may be something else: the fact that Americans want just about everything, without considering or fully understanding the cost. We want freedom as well as order, individual liberty as well as equality, safety as well as the benefits of risk taking, a wide-open society as well as less crime, material wealth as well as spiritual worth—without stopping to think that each of these values takes something away from the other. To use an ungainly but accurate word, we have forgotten the trade-offs.

At home, the most urgent area of renewal is, of course, the economy: curbing inflation by restoring productivity and by limiting government spending. The solution to this all too familiar problem lies in politics more than in economics: Can American democracy, or any modern democracy, restrain the excessive demands made on the society? Can the drift toward the welfare state and egalitarianism be halted without betraying the ideal of social justice? To accomplish this—and everything else we need and want—one thing is essential: sustained economic growth. This means rejecting the disastrous gospel that growth is impossible or wrong, and that small is always beautiful. Moreover, we should keep in mind that socialist, rigidly planned economies are in deep trouble almost everywhere. These matters are examined in several articles in Fortune and Money magazines.

The second great task of renewal involves our political system, which sometimes alarmingly recalls the creeping paralysis of the Third and Fourth French republics. The goal must be once again to strengthen the presidency, to undo some of the misguided reforms that have made Congress so unmanageable, to curb the monstrous federal bureaucracy and to counter the power of single-issue constituencies. Contrary to some critics, we believe that much of this can be accomplished without major changes in the Constitution. We also see the need for revitalizing the political parties and for limited changes in our electoral system, which has been distorted by, among other factors, the questionable notion that the best thing for democracy is more democracy. These issues are examined by Time.

As for the renewal of American power in the world, a subject also treated by Time, it will depend on certain changes in attitude. When it has not been actively intervening, America has viewed its influence abroad as somehow automatic, simply radiating outward through the shining example of the country's strength and goodness. If this was ever true, it surely no longer is. If we Americans want to be a power in the world, we will have to pay for it—and not only in money. For example, it is difficult for a country to be taken seriously as a world power if it refuses to have a military draft in an era of obvious crisis. The U.S.

CHAPTER FOUR
Sports Symbols: *The Radio Times*

RADIO TIMES, the official organ of the British Broadcasting Corporation, was first published in 1923, and is thus exactly the same age as *Time* magazine. One of the attractions of working at *Time* for me was the amazing similarity in the working methods at the two publications. (There is definitely a type of journalist who works toward a weekly deadline, trying to plan ahead and be orderly, but who is still working around the clock on the last night; that animal is the same across the world.)

The difference between the two magazines, however, is basic. While *Time* as a general rule reports the news, *Radio Times* previews events and the programs that the BBC is putting out to cover those events. *Radio Times* was an illustrated paper from the start, employing many of the best illustrators of the time in England, and I was proud to be part of a long tradition. Its name belies the fact that *Radio Times* now covers the BBC's television broadcasting as well and that the features in the magazine take some of the forthcoming programs as a jumping-off point for really detailed examinations of subjects, which stand quite independently from the programs they herald.

The symbols that had preceded my efforts were not really symbolic at all. In fact they were more like tiny illustrations, and although there existed plenty of examples of the type of drawings that I did, it was not until David Driver became art editor in 1969, and asked me to freelance for him, that the magazine used symbolic, as opposed to illustrative, signage in its program listings.

The symbols I designed for the *Radio Times* during the years 1970 through 1978 represented a different type of symbol problem from those I regularly solve at *Time*. The latter are conceived from a newsman's angle to comment on an event or situation and generally demand some sort of editorial judgment. The *Radio Times* symbols, however, do not. Here, there is no editorial angle, no judgment that this is "good show jumping" nor that "golf is a silly game." Rather, the sports symbols simply serve as road signs in the pages of the magazine: "Here is the tennis."

Designers of sports symbols are fortunate indeed, for they have been enriched by a legacy of

WINTER OLYMPICS

SOUTH WEST
7–13 February 1976   Price 10p

Radio Times

Ice queen

Back feature:
Dianne de Leeuw lives in Los Angeles, has a British trainer, but skates for Holland. She is the favourite for the figure-skating gold medal at the Winter Olympics — full coverage all week, BBC1 and Radio 2

INNSBRUCK
1976

Olympian proportions: every four years, as part of preparations for summer and winter Olympic Games, a new set of symbols has been created to indicate both a multitude of sports and an array of visitor and athlete services.

But Olympic symbols are developed to meet rather traditional considerations of symbol-signing: they are designed for a number of uses, ranging from printed matter to large illuminated signboards. While, visually speaking, the symbols I designed for the London *Radio Times* fall clearly within the vernacular of traditional sports imagery, they also satisfy some very different requirements.

Although its name predates the television era, the *Radio Times* provides British radio listeners and television viewers with a complete schedule of BBC programming. Published weekly, the guide is about the size of a typical American Sunday supplement; it is printed in both black-and-white and color sections, in thirteen regional editions.

Sports are very popular with both listening and viewing audiences in Great Britain, especially when summer arrives. With one major competitor for sports coverage, the BBC finds it important to "sell" its sports programming to a degree far greater than its drama, variety, or talk–show programs.

In 1969, as part of the redesign of the *Radio Times* format, art director David Driver, now art director of the London *Times*, wanted to update the symbols used with the various listings in the program guide. I had worked with David for four years on other projects, and it was part of this continuing relationship that he called on me from time to time to design a symbol for the *Radio Times*.

Before the redesign, the programming highlights had been marked with small drawings that were fairly pictorial in aspect. One early one, dating from 1947, was actually a delicate engraving of boxing gloves (1); two from 1965 (2, 3), depicting horse racing and show jumping, were sweet but unconnected. Thus, the *Radio Times* already had a solid tradition of symbol use before I arrived on the scene, and the first symbols I designed more or less carried on that tradition.

Rather than being organized into a true symbol

system, these first symbols were developed on an individual basis, which gave the magazine a rather haphazard look. Only gradually did it become obvious that it would be better to organize the images into a series with one overall style. Since each new sports season was heralded by a cover corner bar with the words "Special Summer of Sports" or some such statement, it was only fitting that a fresh group of symbols be developed for the inside. Thus, year after year, I was asked to redesign existing symbols to do essentially the same job.

Although individual solutions may have varied in scale in earlier years, later symbols were never reproduced larger than one–half inch. (Here they are shown larger for the sake of clarity.) And, while size alone precluded the use of a great deal of detail, I also had to consider certain printing limitations. The paper used in the listings section where the symbols appeared was of a quality similar to newsprint, and it printed only in black.

Given these considerations, I gradually worked toward a cohesive group of symbols. Until 1976, individual styles and imagery prevailed, with each symbol being designed as needed on a problem/ solution basis. But as these discrete solutions began accumulating, the need for more organization became apparent, and in 1976 the first more or less complete set appeared. While still somewhat inconsistent in visual vocabulary, the *Radio Times* had for the first time a set of sports symbols with a marked cohesiveness.

After 1976, the needs of a prevailing symbol language—the language of the set—became a prime consideration in the development of each sports symbol. In 1977, this language was obviously influenced by the symbols designed for the 1976 Olympiad. However, even during these two years, the symbols were prepared on an individual basis. It wasn't until 1978 that I conceived and designed a complete set of *Radio Times* sports symbols, and these are still in use today. Following nine years of precedent, these images are greatly simplified, giving the reader only the barest detail needed to identify the sport being signalled. In this respect, the whole history of the *Radio Times* sports symbols fairly well parallels the development of the broader field of symbol design and a growing public acceptance of symbolic imagery.

GOLF

IN MY EARLY DAYS with the *Radio Times*, when not many symbols were used, symbols could be large and free-wheeling, with type run around. Thus, many of the symbols from that time are more vital and diverse in nature. In the case of the golf symbols, all were basically plays on the image of the golf ball and a club or a tee.

1, 4, 6. These three solutions are variations of the same view—a white golf ball contrasted against a dark club.

2. This design highlighted the texture of a golf ball seen in close-up upon a tee. Interestingly, this solution was not popular with our readers, some of whom saw in it sexual connotations; this only shows that people see what they want to see!

3. A less successful version, this head-on solution is hard to read.

5. A printer's golf ball. Here the dimples, which were made with a graduated screen, added a feeling of roundness.

7. Also produced with a screen, this is the only symbol in the series to make reference to the object of the game—getting the ball into the hole.

8. Designed in the more active language of an overall set of symbols, this is the only one of the golf series that did not focus on the ball.

9. Here, all detail of the ball has disappeared and, with the addition of the tee, the image says "golf" both simply and eloquently.

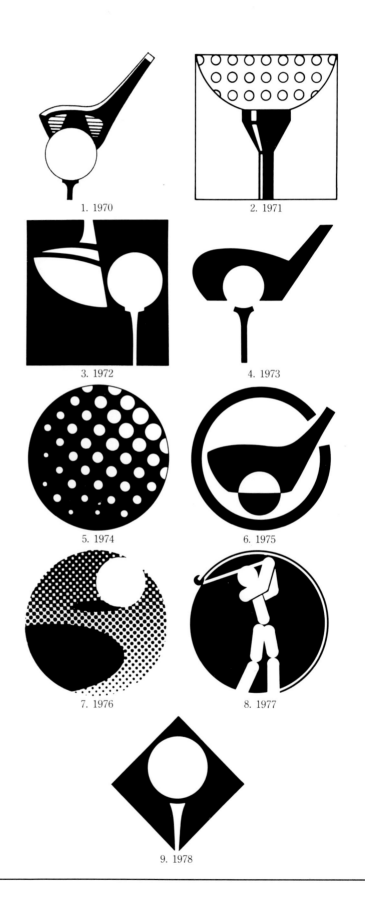

1. 1970

2. 1971

3. 1972

4. 1973

5. 1974

6. 1975

7. 1976

8. 1977

9. 1978

HORSE RACING

THE TWO SPORTS involving horses—racing and show jumping—had to be clearly distinguished in the pages of the *Radio Times*.

1. This is the very first symbol I designed for the *Radio Times*, and in retrospect it doesn't seem special enough. The horse's leg and hoof say "horse" but not "racing," and the symbol really could have been used to indicate practically anything about horses.

2. A simple but realistic silhouette of galloping legs and hooves, this solution was developed in reaction to the previous one.

3. This was an attempt to show the class aspects of the spectator crowd at Royal Ascot, which the Queen and members of Britain's upper crust attend. The horse silhouette here is taken from a pre-Muybridge horse-in-motion photograph and is not locomotively correct. However, its old-fashioned look works well to evoke the traditional nature of the sport.

4, 5, 7, 8. Each of these four images takes advantage of the classic "horse" symbol—a horse's head. With the addition of a top hat or a crown, the head indicates a "royal" race.

6, 10. Both of these symbols use the traditional British finishing-post in conjunction with a horse to indicate horse racing. The earlier solution also represents the first time an overall symbol shape, in this case a square, suggested itself through an experimentation with negative and positive imagery, and thus marks the beginning of a real symbology for the *Radio Times*.

9. By contorting the body of the jockey and including his whip, I was able to distinguish between racing and show jumping in the pin-man designs.

1. 1970

2. 1970

3. 1971

4. 1972

5. 1972

6. 1974

7. 1976

8. 1976

9. 1977

10. 1978

TENNIS

LIKE MANY Radio Times symbols, those designed for this sport focused (with one exception) on the qualities of the ball used to play it.

1. Here a press-on screen lends the ball a three-dimensionality. In use, the symbol was rotated as it was dropped into the text, and when more than one ball appeared on a spread, they appeared to be bouncing across the page. The same positioning technique was not so successful with the other "ball solutions" (3–5) because—although the balls were round—their starkness made them seem less real.

2. The earth as a tennis ball, this symbol surely must qualify as the smallest map of the world: as it appeared in the *Radio Times*, it measured only one-quarter inch across and was meant to indicate "world tennis."

3. Conceived in reaction to the "reality" of earlier designs, this symbol is from what one of my teachers called the "bent pin" school of symbol design: a single line is bent around to describe a shape.

4. This symbol fails because, in an attempt to be different, I colored the ball black. Here, the end did not justify the means: in visual language, a tennis ball somehow must always be white.

5. Here, the by-now-familiar "S" of the tennis ball is set against a grid pattern that suggests the strings of a net or racquet.

6. This symbol focuses on the participant and is consistent with the other pin-man figures developed in 1977.

7. Presaged by figure 5, this solution is simplified in terms of the language of the group designed that year (1978).

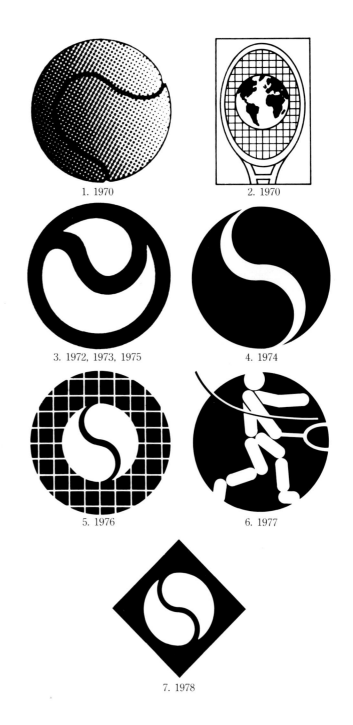

1. 1970

2. 1970

3. 1972, 1973, 1975

4. 1974

5. 1976

6. 1977

7. 1978

SHOW JUMPING

As a child this sport was a passion of mine, so these symbols gave me an excuse as an adult to continue an involvement with horses, even if I was only drawing them!

1. The first image used the same visual language as the horse racing symbol of the year: the form of a horse in active silhouette.

2,4. The simple side-view silhouette became much more stylized, and a striped rail drawn in perspective added visual interest, especially in 4, where the angle of the rail is quite extreme.

3,5. It is much harder to achieve a successful graphic shape with a three-quarter view of the subject, and these two solutions, notably 3, are rather too complicated.

6. This symbol was used for both show-jumping and three-day eventing (cross-country, dressage, and show-jumping events held on separate days), and so I focused on the outdoor aspect of the sport. By using a very upright head there was no confusion with the horse racing symbols of the same year.

7. In the language of that year, this symbol was different from the racing one, while still remaining a figure on a horse. Again, a more upright racing position was the key to achieving this.

8. The final solution was the same horse's head as that of the year's racing symbol, but here the finishing post has been replaced by a pair of jumping rails set outside the symbol frame.

1. 1971

2. 1972

3. 1973

4. 1974

5. 1975

6. 1976

7. 1977

8. 1978

RUGGBY AND SOCCER

In both of these groups, the ball used to play the sport is a significant element; for the soccer symbols, this form is often assisted by a studded soccer-boot.

1. Like others that year (1970), this symbol reveals a lack of discipline in overall shape and is more pictorial than symbolic.

2. A simple shape, designed to be used at different angles on the page, to give it animation.

3. In an attempt to be different, I pictured the ball sailing over a goal post.

4. The pin-man symbol used in 1977 carries the ball toward a touchdown.

5. Like figures 1 and 2, this simple solution relies entirely on the form of the ball to convey its message.

6. This symbol from 1970 features an active, silhouetted figure engaged in the sport.

7, 8, 12. Here, the familiar soccer ball meets the studded boot. This imagery, which began early on, survived until the final set (1978).

9. A visual pun: a map of Britain wears a soccer boot to signify the "Home Internationals," a soccer series in which England, Northern Ireland, Scotland, and Wales play one another.

10. Like the tennis symbol of the same year (1976), this soccer ball is headed into the net.

11. The pin-man takes his turn at football.

1. 1976

2. 1975

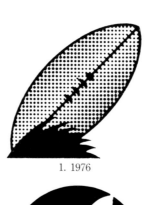

3. 1976

4. 1977

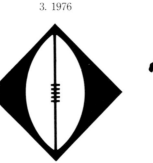

5. 1978

6. 1970

7. 1971

8. 1972

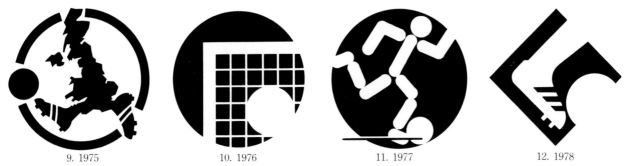

9. 1975

10. 1976

11. 1977

12. 1978

ATHLETICS AND GYMNASTICS

BEFORE 1975, only two symbols had been designed to highlight athletic (track and field) meets; until 1976, no gymnastics symbol had been used at all. That a gymnastics symbol was called for was due to the fact that the sport became terrifically popular after the Russian gymnast Olga Korbut introduced her "dancing" style at the Munich Olympics in 1972; interest escalated again after Nadia Comaneci appeared in the 1976 Games.

1, 2. In referring to the medals traditionally awarded to the first, second, and third-place winners of track and field events, both of these symbols were somewhat ambiguous and might be taken to mean any athletic competition.

3, 5. The running figure developed in 1975 was a much more accurate athletics symbol, and the stripes across the chest, which at the time was part of the uniform for British athletes, made the symbol recognizable as more than just a running person. Figure 5 is the 1977 pin-man version of figure 3.

4, 6. Two varieties of a single idea that I feel is the best solution in the series: a track shoe pressing into the starting line. This image is neither too specific nor too general and, because it's better than the others graphically, it's also more enduring.

7. Since gymnastics includes a number of events that may be performed by only men, only women, or athletes of either sex, it is difficult to find a single image to represent them all. This one is based on a men's event—the horse vault.

8. With the arrival of Korbut and Comaneci, women's events became the big attraction, and the balletic movement of this figure was a direct reference to this fact.

9. Finally an asexual symbol: a figure poised above a single bar that could stand for the men's high parallel bars or the women's high-low bars.

1. 1971

2. 1974

3. 1975

4. 1976

5. 1977

6. 1978

7. 1976

8. 1977

9. 1978

WHEELED SPORTS

THIS GROUP INCLUDES symbols for several sports, including bicycle and motorcycle racing and auto racing and rallying. They all come together in the final symbol, which focuses not on the individual conveyance but on a common goal: the finish line.

1. Designed for the Tour de France, this symbol is a literal close-up of a cyclist's foot strapped into a pedal.

2. Most symbols work best in profile, and this three-quarter abstraction of a racing motorcycle, drawn from a low angle, is particularly hard to read. It's not a true symbol, but a drawing reduced to light and shadow. Significantly, for this solution I felt it necessary to include the suggestion of a boxed symbol shape.

3. While this section of a racing car is quite literal, it shows too little of the object to be easily identified. Here, I really hadn't thought through what would be symbolic for this sport and simply tried to force the long, low shape of a racing car into the boxy shape of a symbol.

4. A racer's Darth Vader-like helmet is a better symbol in a graphic sense but conveys little of the excitement of the sport.

5. This symbol for rallying is better than the car section used in figure 3, but it's still too contrived and too pictorial. Its most successful element is the special cluster of rally lights on the front of the car.

6. A more graphic version of figure 5, this symbol for rallying is still not successful. However, the use of a black background that could be read as a night sky suggests the 24-hour aspect of rally driving and also imparts a stronger shape to the image.

7, 8. Presaged in figure 7, the checkered flag in figure 8 is the definitive symbol for this sport; in comparison, all previous symbols were really drawings of individual racing events.

1. 1970

2. 1971

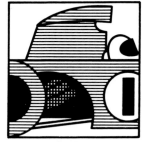

3. 1972

4. 1973

5. 1973

6. 1976

7. 1977

8. 1978

BOXING, POOL, AND TABLE TENNIS

WITH THE EXCEPTION of the symbol for the Ali–Lewis boxing match, the symbols in this group were developed late in my tenure with the *Radio Times*, and they work within the specified symbol imagery of the sets of which they were a part.

1. The Ali–Lewis bout in 1972 was big enough to warrant a symbol of its own. The legendary mouth shouts for itself.

2. This figure of a boxer was also designed for a specific bout, but was later used as a generic boxing symbol.

3. As demonstrated so many times, the simplest symbol is often the best. And what could say "boxing" more simply than a glove?

4. By 1977, pool, or "snooker" as it's called in England, became popular enough as a TV sport to get its own symbol, here designed in the then-current pin-man image.

5. The final pool symbol was derived directly from the configuration of the game.

6. The first table-tennis symbol appeared in 1977, and the pin-man used that year helped establish the correct proportions of the game. Although this symbol could not be mistaken for "tennis," it still carries a certain ambiguity.

7. Less ambiguous is this simpler image of a ball and paddle, which is still slightly confusing because of the play of its negative-positive imagery.

1. 1972

2. 1974, 1976

3. 1978

4. 1977

5. 1978

6. 1977

7. 1978

ICE SPORTS

In England, the term "ice sports" most often means figure skating. However, in 1976 I designed a group of symbols to mark the *Radio Times'* coverage of events in the Winter Olympics, and these figures included other sports as well. Throughout the series, I kept returning to a screened background that lent a cold starkness to the foreground figure.

1. In the fashion of the golf and rugby symbols of that year (1970), this first image for skating is large and free-wheeling. I still like it: the white boot of the skate seems right for this graceful but exciting sport, and compared with figure 3, which is better graphically, this first effort has far more vitality.

2. The skating figure designed for the European Figure Skating Championships in 1973 is really a piece of ice calligraphy. It was modified for use with Olympic coverage in 1976.

3. A generic symbol for use with non-Olympic events in 1976.

4–9. This set of pictograms was designed to highlight coverage of the 1976 Winter Olympics.

10. The skating pin-man with speed-lines and the merest suggestion of skates was designed in the vernacular of his fellows.

1. 1970

2. 1973

3. 1976

4. 1976

5. 1976

6. 1976

7. 1976

8. 1976

9. 1976

10. 1977

SYMBOL SET: 1976

ALTHOUGH IN 1975 I had begun to think of the *Radio Times* sports symbols in terms of a common circular border, the first visually connected series appeared only in 1976.

This matched set was accomplished by simply deciding to enclose whatever symbol I did in a circular shape. In each case, the image was developed in white so as to "eat into" the black circular background.

However, because each of these symbols was designed individually and in its own imagery, the group does not quite hang together as a "set." Some, like the golf ball rolling into the hole and the treescape appearing behind the head of the show-jumping horse, were especially realistic in imagery; there was no real attempt made to shape the figures within a cohesive pictorial style.

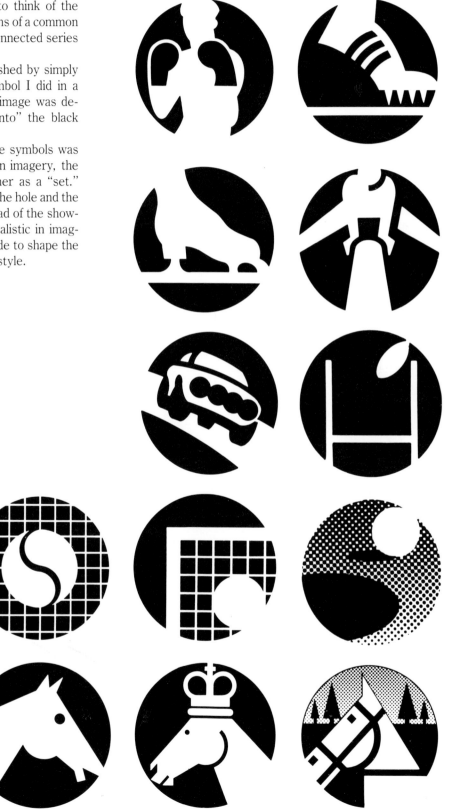

SYMBOL SET: 1977

THIS SERIES TOOK its cue from the official Olympic symbols developed for the 1972 games in Munich, for which I used stick figures engaged in various sports. However, only five of the dozen sports for which I developed symbols during the course of the year were also Olympic sports.

In this group, the pin-man athlete had to be flexible enough in design terms and carry enough detail to play widely disparate sports, whether golf or table tennis or pool. Drawing the symbols was a real test of anatomical articulation.

For each symbol, I started with a rough drawing of a stick figure doing whatever was charac-teristically needed to play the sport. This I traced over with templates using the grammar of the system (1). By keeping the tracings and referring to them as each new symbol was designed, I was able to standardize the size of the figure within the system and maintain the relative scale of its various anatomical parts.

These symbols are particularly effective in the sense that they express the action inherent in sports competition. Occasionally I emphasized this aspect by breaking the symbol's outer circle with a speed-line or with part of the figure itself.

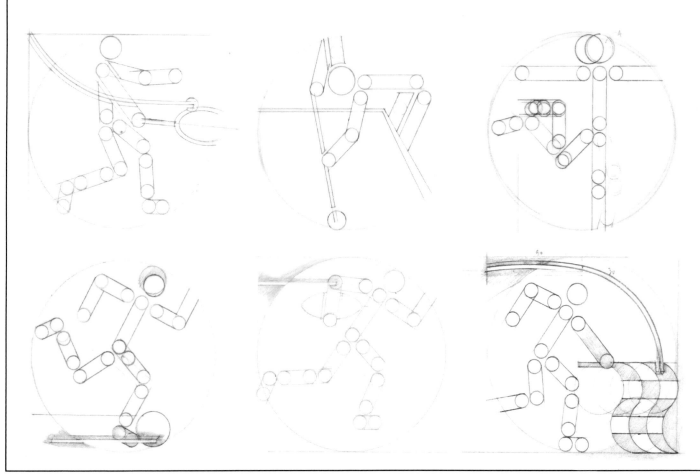

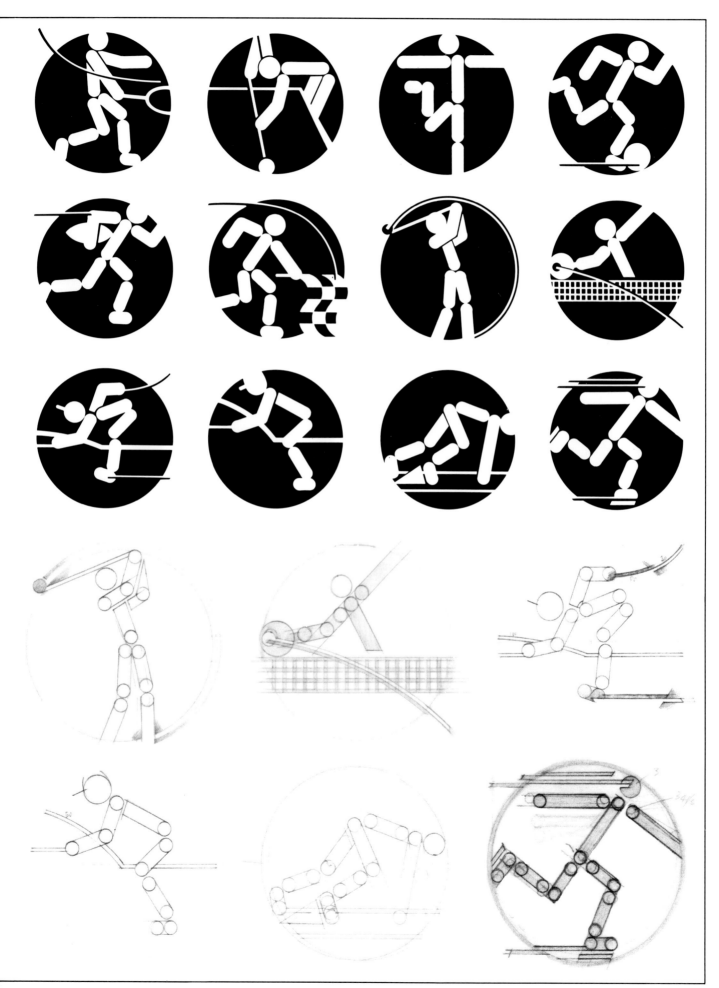

SYMBOL SET: 1978

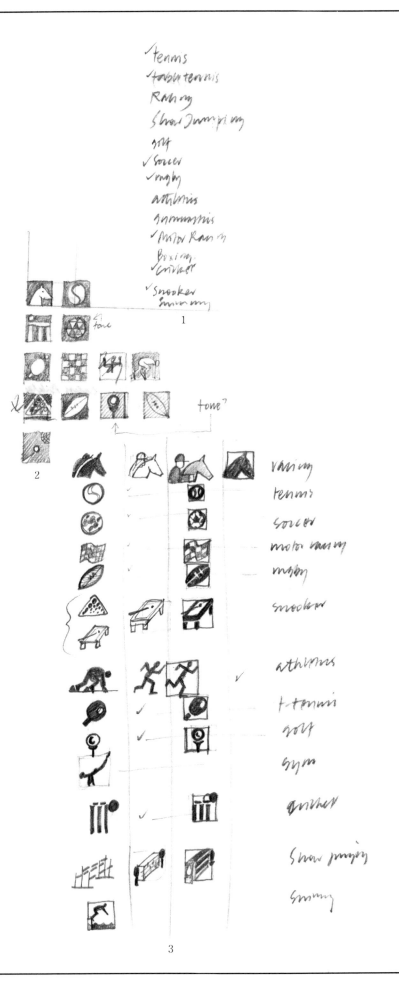

IN 1978, FOR THE first time, I designed a set of *Radio Times* sports symbols that were not executed on a piecemeal basis. Because I knew from the start that I would be designing them all at once and delivering a complete set, I was able to think about the images not only in terms of individual sports but also in terms of how the group would relate as a whole.

To start, I jotted down a checklist of the symbols that would be needed (1) and then made a first attempt at considering an overall shape that would differ from the round symbols of the previous year. I chose a simple square (2). These sketches also started me thinking in terms of alternative designs for the individual symbols, which I further developed in a comparative mode (3) that had more to do with symbol imagery than with overall shape.

From this group I selected those I liked best, as indicated by the small check marks, and drew them as well as some alternatives a bit more tightly in ink (4). However, at this point I was still holding out against any regimented symbol shape. These diverse forms, I felt, would give the *Radio Times* a bright, lively look when scattered across the page. I conceived them to be run very small, so that we could use more of them without creating a sense of clutter. However, this group was not well received by the *Radio Times*, and I headed back to the drawing board.

A brief flirtation with the idea of using hands (5) ended in a coolly rational observation that certain sports—soccer, for example—would be impossible to convey in that language. From there, I returned to the idea of a unifying symbol shape and made some sketches on graph paper (6). In an attempt to create something different from what had been used previously, I conceived a series of symbols to be placed inside oblique parallelograms, which seemed to me a particularly dynamic shape. I went so far as to tighten up these ideas in another set of drawings (7) before I realized that some of the images just didn't fit neatly into that shape. In addition, the parallelogram would be difficult to place into the text.

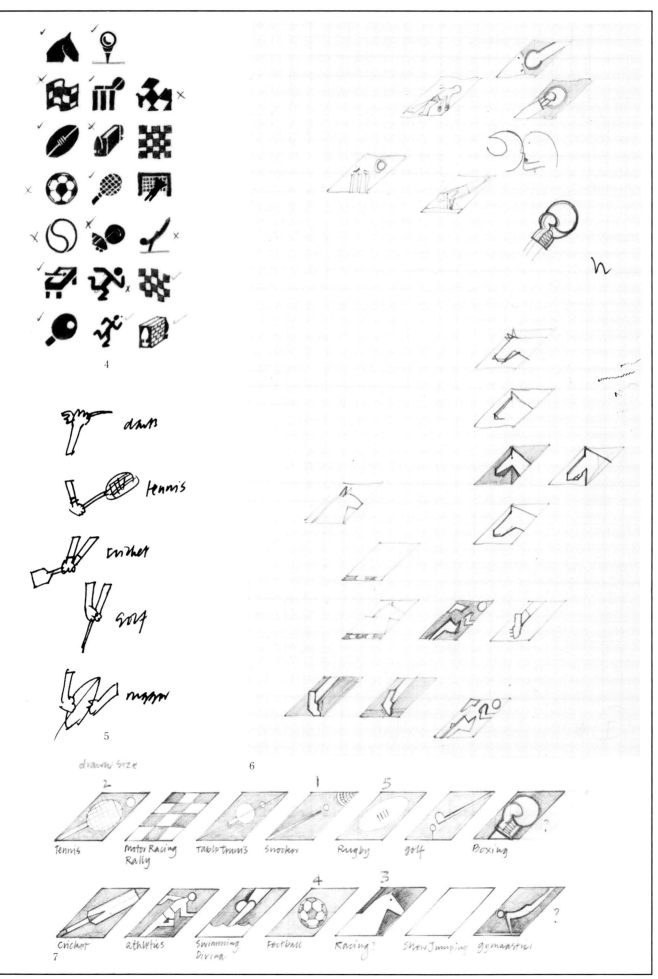

4

darts

tennis

cricket

golf

athletics

5

drawn size

6

2

Tennis

Motor Racing Rally

Table Tennis

Snooker

Rugby

golf

Boxing ?

Cricket

athletics

Swimming Diving

Football

Racing ?

Show Jumping

gymnastics ?

7

127

My next group of sketches (8) substituted a true diamond form for the parallelogram, but this form, while better suited to the developing imagery, was not much more successful when placed into the text. So, I broadened the diamond into a square that had been rotated 90 degrees so as to sit on end (9). This configuration afforded a larger image area and at the same time created a pleasing space around itself on the page. From these small sketches I developed a series of working drawings (10) that were used in preparing the final art (11).

This series of sports symbols has been used by the *Radio Times* since 1978. Its overall vocabulary is uncluttered and starkly black and white: there are no hints at tints. Occasionally I broke my own rules in this group by altering the format; the "pool" symbol, for example, uses the edge of the symbol as the edge of the table, and the two equestrian symbols are distinguished from one another by elements placed outside the symbol frame. Nonetheless, their overall simplicity and economy of style have allowed them to endure.

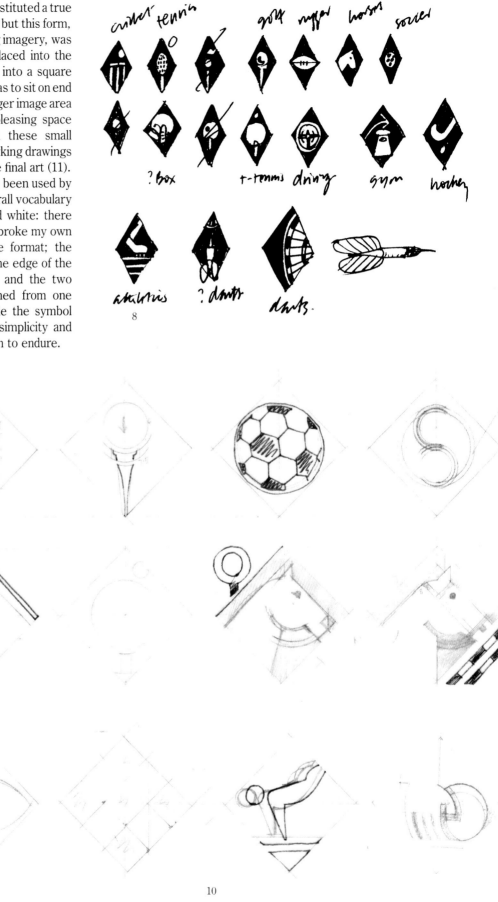

11

CHAPTER FIVE
A Gallery of Symbols

London 1948

ANY COLLECTION of symbols—such as the examples in this chapter—reflects the personal preferences of the gatherer. I like all of the pieces on the following pages and have attempted to say something about each of them to explain why. Included are editorial symbols like those in previous chapters and also some symbols that could be termed trademarks. The price of entry is simple: a pictorial idea—even if in some cases it is based on a letter of the alphabet.

The completely abstract symbol is excluded; there are at least a dozen books currently in print which deal with trademarks, logos, and other signs, so my focus here is deliberately narrower.

No book about pictorial symbols would be complete without some consideration of Olympic symbols. The brief discussion that follows is not a complete treatment of the subject but seeks to highlight certain developments from 1948 to 1984. Undoubtedly, the designers involved in the Tokyo, Mexico, and Munich Olympics (1964–1972) made considerable contributions in terms of advancing the form and the cause of symbolic, non-linguistic signs. Although the visual description of each Olympic sport has great impact, for the sake of comparison, I have taken one example—swimming—to illustrate the evolution of a design.

In 1948, the games were held in London. Some of the "sports" contested then are now obsolete. Art, for instance, was judged in the category of a design for medals and badges. The symbols for the games themselves were, like the heraldic badge that is sewn into a blazer or track suit, not really symbolic at all. The English designers at that time obviously hadn't seen, or were choosing to ignore, the work of Neurath and Modley. Instead, they carried on their own tradition of the embroidered sports emblem, which was much more literal.

The first real pictograms were designed by Katsumie Masaru with Yoshiro Yamashita for the Tokyo games of 1964. For me, they remain the best of the bunch.* In his excellent *Handbook of Pictorial Symbols*, the late Rudolf Modley called Masaru "the major force behind the development of international pictorial and public symbology." The ease with which Masaru achieves his swimming image is stunning. It is a reduction of forms down to the most basic, yet still remains pictorially descriptive of the energy and speed of the sport.

In 1968, for the Mexico games, Lance Wyman, Eduardo Terrazas, and Manuel Villazon gave their

pictographs a holding shape with rounded corners. The shapes inside this overall frame became much more static. In some cases, the symbols had more to do with the equipment used in the sport than with the active participation by athletes.

Probably the best-known Olympic symbols are those by Otl Aicher; designed for the 1972 Munich games, they were used again with slight modifications in 1976 at Montreal. Aicher returned to the human figure as a basis for his set of symbols. His pictographic athletes are much more geometric and stick-like than Masaru's. They conform very strictly to a grid and lack a certain warmth but are extremely efficient and communicative.

Heiner Jacob, an associate of Aicher's, acknowledged the debt the two owed to Masaru: "The Tokyo signs were a basis. However they were constructed unsystematically . . . for Munich there is a constant set of elements: a body alphabet (head, body, arms, and legs). The elements of this alphabet are arranged in a grid of four possible directions: horizontal, vertical, and two diagonal lines."

After the Montreal games of 1976, the International Olympic Committee commissioned Julien van der Wal to design a set of "official" signs that were supposed to become the standard for future years. Van der Wal used a grid of 121 (11 × 11) dots, which could also have been points of light, thereby making use of electronic methods of signage. Much less readable than their predecessors, the symbols were never officially used. For Moscow, in 1980, a system derived from Aicher's Munich/Montreal series was used. However, with the spaces around the elements of the original body language filled in, the figures appeared blurred, which harmed their readability.

In 1984, the Los Angeles games had yet another set of symbols, this time designed by Keith Bright, assisted by Ken Parkhurst and art director Ray Wood. Again based on Aicher's, the Bright symbols were best seen in large sizes, on the banners and other decorative Olympic material that transformed Los Angeles so well into the host city. But they did not print well at a small size, with many tiny, subtle details that were lost in reduction.

As a client, the Olympic games have obviously been important; the individual symbols in the collection that follows may not have taken so long nor been so difficult to design, but as examples of a graphic art form they are all good.

Tokyo 1964

Mexico 1968

Munich 1972
Montreal 1976

"Official" IOC

Moscow 1980

Los Angeles 1984

*Masaru further developed his personal pictorial language with the 1972 Sapporo Winter Olympics.

1. Designed by Harry Murphy, this symbol for the Marin Swim School cleverly combines the letter M and the handrails on the side of a pool to make a distinctive mark.

2. This humanization of a theater ticket by the insertion of two profiles (which do double duty as the tear in the ticket when one is admitted to the performance) is the work of designer Michael Manwaring. The client is Performing Arts Services, Inc. The first three letters of the organization's name (with the addition of a final S) are used as a label on the ticket and reinforce the message of the symbol.

3. For a Japanese bank, Seibu Credit, Ikko Tanaka designed this arresting image of a hand with what may be read as either a target, a stack of coins, or simply a focusing device, to draw attention to the human aspects of banking.

4. A symbol designed by Nigel Holmes for the New Opportunity Press emphasizes the first step on the ladder to success. The shadow under the shoe gives this design a little extra depth and subtly suggests that the step is about to be taken, rather than that the foot has been firmly planted on the ladder. Thus it is a sign that indicates help for those who are looking for a job, not for those who already have one.

5. Joe Aslaender created this portrait of a colleague in the art department at *Time* magazine on a Typositor photosetting machine, by manipulating Franklin Gothic characters, punctuation marks, and accents until a cartoon likeness was achieved.

6. The Iranian graphic artist Morteza Momayez designed a variation on the traditional laughing and crying masks for the Azad Theatre Group. The economy of means and reduction of the original symbolic masks to the barest essentials are very effective.

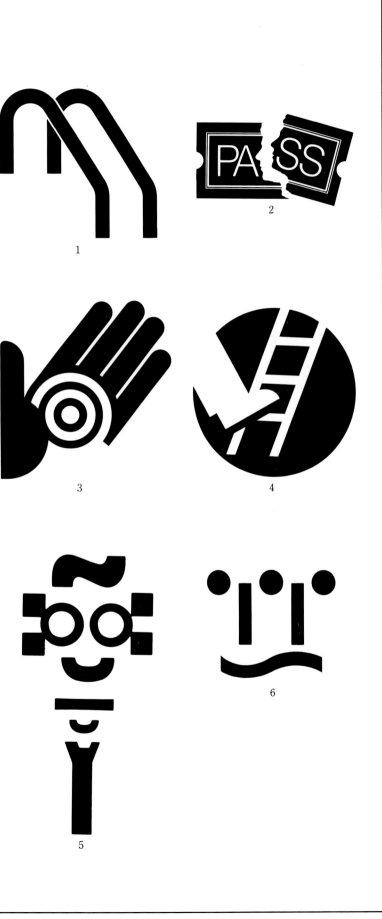

7. Five images from a calendar for a phototypesetting company show with what simple means well-known faces can be created. From the top: Charlie Chaplin, Carmen Miranda, W.C. Fields, Groucho Marx, Harold Lloyd. All were designed from basic typographic elements by John McConnell, of Pentagram, for Face Photosetting.

8. John McConnell, of Pentagram, created this symbol for an aircraft designer, using the light touch of calligraphy to suggest both the idea of designing and the object designed.

9. The brilliant Japanese graphic artist Shigeo Fukuda specializes in optical illusion and other graphic tricks. He states that this mark is for a health-insurance poster, but it is included here for its wonderful interplay of shapes (which do you see first?) more than for the appropriateness of its application.

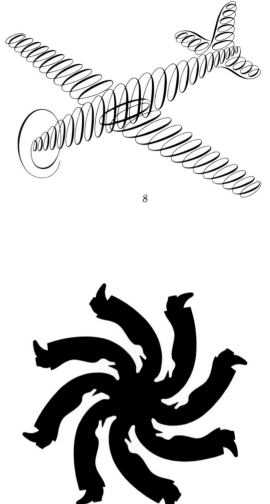

8

10. This is a really terrific set of symbols for the National Zoological Park; the symbols display a remarkable consistency, while never becoming boring by adhering too rigidly to a set of rules. The limited use of pattern and the few fine lines that do appear (whiskers, for instance) add just the right touch of wit. Note the slight but telling difference in the shape and size of the various eyes. It would have been easy to have used a standard circle, but these eyes really capture the essence of the animals. The last symbol in the series is the overall mark for the zoo itself. In picturing an adult eagle feeding its young, it symbolizes the continuation of species. The zoo says: "Our mission is not just to preserve individuals, but also to preserve the succession of generations." It is obvious from this work that the designers—Bill Cannon, Robert E. Mulcahy, and Lance Wyman—care a lot about animals, too.

9

11. An interesting illusion of depth is created in this symbol of overlapping faces, designed by Katsuichi Ito, for Kokusai Securities Co. The tradition of both heraldic and family devices in Japan is a beneficial heritage for designers there today.

12. This sign system for a store in Japan utilizes a fairly uniform, thick line to describe the shapes. They are bold, simple but sophisticated, and nicely balanced between black and white. The symbols were designed by Kazumasa Nagai for the Nichii Co., Ltd.

7

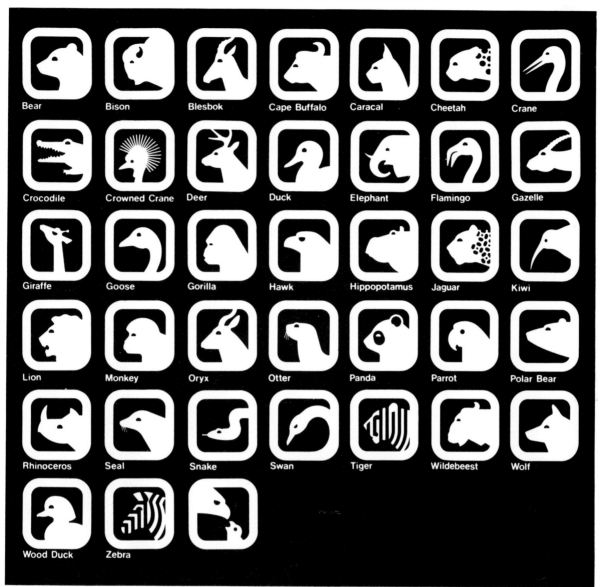

Bear Bison Blesbok Cape Buffalo Caracal Cheetah Crane

Crocodile Crowned Crane Deer Duck Elephant Flamingo Gazelle

Giraffe Goose Gorilla Hawk Hippopotamus Jaguar Kiwi

Lion Monkey Oryx Otter Panda Parrot Polar Bear

Rhinoceros Seal Snake Swan Tiger Wildebeest Wolf

Wood Duck Zebra

10

11

12

13. For Hearst Publications, designer Dan Silverstone drew this book with two notches cut out of the cover to form the letter H. The perspective view of the book gives an elegant edge to this crisp symbol.

14. Designer Isao Bingo used a pencil to represent education in this symbol for the Sk Gakuin Educational Research Co. in Japan. He bent the pencil into a figure eight to indicate overlapping pathways, or routes, to education. The use of the facets of the pencil as contours on the "road" is a neat double-use of a graphic element.

15. Unlike most of the examples here, this nice symbol for The Green Thumb Plant Store is pictorially intricate and literal, but is nonetheless very good. The lines of the fingerprint mimic furrows in the ground, or at least an engraved image of that ground, and the white shape within the fingerprint is at once a shadow on the ground and a suggestion that the leaf/tree grew out of some magic touch from the "green" finger. The symbol was designed by Steven Sessions.

16. This symbol was designed by Christo Aleksiev for the letters column in a Bulgarian women's magazine. Very simple and straightforward, it somehow evokes a female shape without forcing anything.

17. Designed by Infield D'Astolfo Associates for the Parental Stress Center, this well-organized symbol utilizes a mechanical style to portray a sensitive situation very well. If parents go to a stress center because they cannot cope with their little ones, this little picture should remind them that they are, after all, the grown-ups and that their children are pretty helpless without them.

18. The symbol for a business specializing in sailing equipment makes elegant use of a twisted-rope motif. The symmetry of the design is an effective way of organizing what could have become an unruly knot. It was designed by Michael Vanderbyl, of Vanderbyl Design.

13

14

15

16

17

18

19. In perhaps the most provocative symbol in this section, Steven Session's mark for Star Semen graphically shows the parts of the bull's anatomy that are the basic equipment used by the company.

20. This endearing sign for an animal medical clinic in Albuquerque, New Mexico, neatly combines two slightly clichéd images into one memorable design, by Maggie Macnab.

21. Variations on the male and female signs abound. But then they are instantly recognizable, and when teamed up with other graphic elements, they communicate very quickly. Thus we know this pen nib represents something female even before we discover that it is, in fact, for the International Women's Writing Guild. It was designed by Bruce Zahor.

22. An ingenious twist on the female sign is this symbol for the Women's Auxiliary of the American Institute of Architects. The T-square is a brilliant touch—true to its own shape, but also echoing a pair of shoulders so well. It was designed by Mark Moore of 3D/International Graphic Design.

23. In four related symbols for a *Fortune* magazine article about the stock prices of several hospital service companies, designer Joe Lertola reduced all the shapes to a single, simple line, a device that unifies the diverse subjects to be shown in the group.

24. Some countries are a godsend to the graphic designer; they have a national symbol that quite simply *says* that country every time you see it. Canada is one such place, and this maple-leaf racquet, created by Yoshi Sekiguchi, of Rising Sun Design, is a perfect example of the joining together of two images to make a witty mark. The client was the Maple Leaf Racquet Club.

25. Ice-hockey pucks are not striped, but the referees' sweaters are; the two ideas put together produce this very good symbol for the Colorado Ice Hockey Referees Association. Designed by Pam Jones, it is a very strong image.

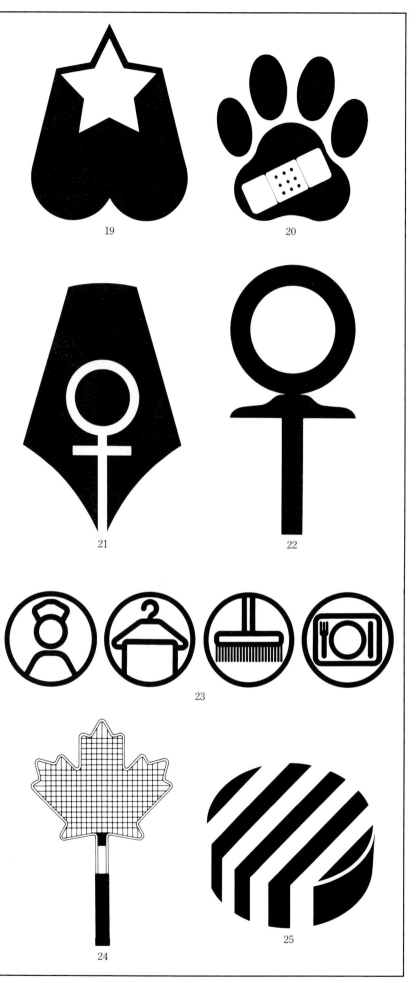

19

20

21

22

23

24

25

26. Designer Abraham Amuny and artist Larry McIntyre made this symbol out of the initial letter of their client, Shults Construction Co. It works well, so long as you are not too literal-minded about the sort of nails they are going to use on your house!

27. For the Society of Environmental Designers, a symbol that looks like a road sign is particularly appropriate. Doug Akagi, Richard Burns and Jeffry Corbin gave the classic pictographic man an arrow to carry, and they printed it in black with a yellow background to further underline the road-sign connection.

28. Taking a line for a walk around two faces is a good graphic solution to this symbol for the Pittsburgh Psychoanalytic Center. It was designed by Frank D'Astolfo, with artist Richard McGarrity. As with many symbols, the meaning is to a certain extent in the eye of the beholder. I take this one to refer to two sides of a personality.

29. The particular shape of a racquetball paddle is the overall format for this friendly sign, designed for the Sunset Racquet Club by Gary Alfredson. The joyful little figure with outstretched arms makes this a very lively mark.

30. This is a variation on the familiar theatrical masks (see also 6). The laughing mask, drawn in profile, casts a shadow which becomes the tragic mask. Designed by Pentagram, in competition with others for the British National Theatre, this symbol was not adopted by the client.

31. In an evocation of the spy-hole in the door, this symbol for the Speakeasy Club uses a large screen-size halftone of an eye peeping through. The image, by Pentagram, is reminiscent of a newspaper's coarse reproduction: that was the way most people saw gangster images in the twenties and thirties. The screen size also ensures that the symbol can be reduced without clogging up; in fact, the design is really all "line-work," but with the effect of a real photo instead of a graphically simplified eye.

26

27

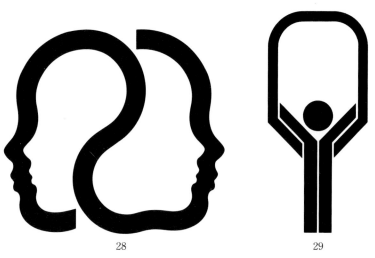

28

29

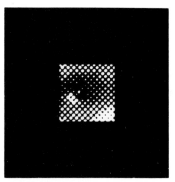

30

31

32. The forerunner of many symbols utilizing the British Union Jack, this mark by Pentagram was for British Trade Weeks, a government scheme for promoting products abroad. The clever use of the central bands of the flag as the ribbons tying up the box enabled the designer to play off some free-wheeling shapes against the rigid, straight lines of the flag proper.

33. Echoing the winding band on traditional Arab headdress, this symbol for the Conference of Islamic Solidarity held in Saudi Arabia is made up of six crescents, one for each Islamic country. The illusion of three dimensions is clever, for the crescent shapes are completely symmetrical and flat. This too was designed by Pentagram.

34. Old and new graphic forms are combined in an effort to reflect the established and traditional values of a firm of real-estate agents operating today. The familiar handshake, signifying agreement and the completion of a sale, was drawn in a deliberately old-fashioned way but was then framed by a modern pictogram for a house, to bring it up to date. This was designed for B. L. Wells and Sons, England, by Nigel Holmes.

35. David Grimsrud's nice letter-R-with-dog strikes just the right note for the Rochester Kennel Club. As in Shigeo Fukuda's work (see number 9), the viewer's eye bounces back and forth between background and foreground; sometimes the R is more prominent, sometimes the dog.

36. The letter W (for West End Studio) forms a neat workspace for the two artists shown in this symbol designed by John Casado and artist Calvin Hom. Simple silhouettes make this a very dramatic black-and-white image.

37. Timo Turjas, from Finland, designed this nicely literal symbol for a clothes-transport company. The multiple-hanger idea conveys the sense of large numbers of items being moved around.

38. A symbol by Nigel Holmes for a program against alcohol abuse in England places a bottle in the counter of the letter A. The label is positioned deliberately to coincide with the crossbar of the letter.

39. For Sentry Medical Products, designer Mike Quon chose a capsule as the basic shape and background for his highly stylized pictograph of a human. There is real drama in the arrow pointing straight up at the head and in the use of positive and negative shapes.

32

33

34

35

36

37

38

39

40. To accompany a magazine's regular column about night-life, this simplified cat, out for the night, was placed on a wall exactly where its tail could also be the moon. It was drawn by Nigel Holmes for Charlie Riddell, art director of *Ohio Life* magazine.

41. In a symbol developed in the late sixties for the British Broadcasting Corporation's Reading Program, a uniform thickness of line is made to describe the figure of a person holding a book. It can be greatly reduced and is used often in the pages of the *Radio Times*, just like the sports symbols described in that section.

42. This page from a 1942 agricultural almanac is included here to remind us of a time when printers used a mass of tiny pictorial symbols in pages of type. The symbols were in fact included in the metal type used for letterpress printing and were set along with the rest of the type. Shown here are characters for the constellational signs of the zodiac (Taurus, Aquarius, Pisces, Aries, Gemini, and so on), the planets and their aspects, and the phases of the moon—all completely integrated with the type, but very economical of space and beautiful to look at, too. It was published by John Baer's Sons Inc., Lancaster, Pennsylvania.

43. Two related signs were produced by Jann Church Advertising and Graphic Design, Inc.— one for MLA/Interiors (left) one for MLA/Haus (right). One division of the MLA organization deals with interior design; the other division deals with construction and remodeling. These simple marks convey both the general framework (the home) and the different services offered. The hammer is especially pleasing.

44. Ron Sullivan's design for the Dallas Services for the Visually Impaired makes good use of the heart as the iris of an eye formed by two caring, sympathetic hands. The fingers as eyelashes are a particularly nice touch.

45. The symbol by Jann Church for the Bixby Ranch is a dramatically simple rendition of barbed wire—unfortunately an important feature in the life of people who want to keep animals in, and others out.

40   41

42

43   44

45

46. For the National Aquarium in Baltimore, Tom Geismar designed this Escher-like water/fish pattern. Lively and light, it captures the spirit of a place where people go to be both entertained and taught.

47. This really compact drawing of fork, spoon, and knife was designed by Mario Righetto for the Association of Suppliers of Silver Plated Cutlery. The way the sides of the spoon also serve as a part of the fork and of the knife makes this a most successful symbol.

48. The *Times* of London uses a great many pictorial symbols in its columns; most are drawn by John Grimwade under the art direction of David Driver. On the left is a symbol to go with a story about how the time of year that a child is born affects its chances of getting asthma (summer and autumn are bad). On the right, for a piece about health hazards in the garden, is a wonderfully simple abstraction of a thorn. Very much to the point!

49. Robert Lockwood's News Graphics and Computer Graphics companies have produced great quantities of pictorial symbols in the course of their work on charts and information pieces for the Associated Press. This well-related group of symbols, drawn by Gerry Chapleski, accompanied a story on the break-up of AT&T; it is notable that the artist was confident enough of his drawings not to rely on strong blacks and other graphic contrasts, but instead was happy to let them be simple line drawings. They are all the better for that restraint.

50. Herbert Bayer edited and designed the *World Geo-Graphic Atlas*, which was published in 1953, for the Container Corporation of America. These tiny map symbols, just a very few of the huge number used in the atlas, are classic examples of the control and consistency needed for this type of design. They are clear and precise, yet varied enough to be interesting without being confusing. (In the preface, Bayer says: "This book is called *World Geo-Graphic Atlas* because it includes, in addition to GEO-graphic maps, many GRAPHIC illustrations of subjects closely related to modern geography.")

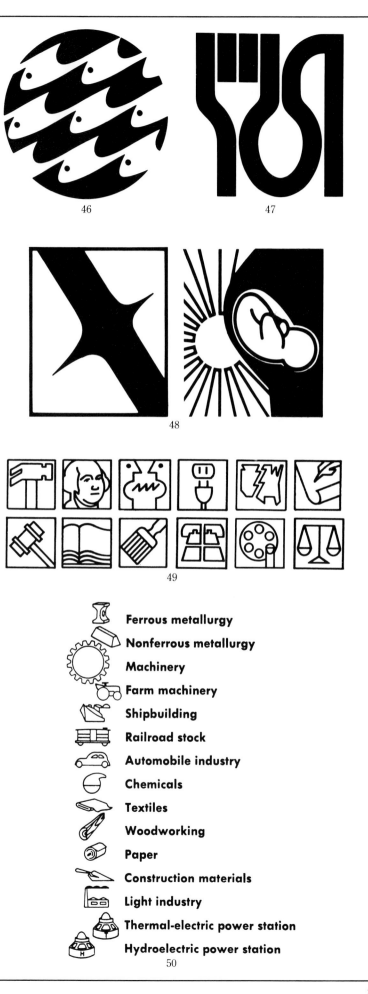

46

47

48

49

Ferrous metallurgy
Nonferrous metallurgy
Machinery
Farm machinery
Shipbuilding
Railroad stock
Automobile industry
Chemicals
Textiles
Woodworking
Paper
Construction materials
Light industry
Thermal-electric power station
Hydroelectric power station

50

The following four examples are all by Daniel Pelavin, who uses many of the techniques of simplification described in this book. His work is clean, symbolic, beautifully drawn, and bright—even in black!

51. A series of symbols for *Travel and Leisure* magazine was used to illustrate an article about the prices of goods and services in different countries. Top row: a hotel room and alcoholic beverage. Middle row: lunch and coffee. Bottom row: transportation and taxi fares. They were originally printed in a variety of colors.

52. For *Progressive Grocer* magazine, this symbol was one of thirty used for an article about the variety of non-edible things sold in supermarkets.

53. A good example that not all symbols should be constructed solely from straight lines or perfect circles, this is from a feature in *McCalls* about health.

54. This italicized factory conveys very quickly and wittily the impression of a successful operation making lots of money—or burning it; then again, the factory could be polluting the atmosphere expensively. Well, I did say that some symbols were open to interpretation!

55. The award certificate for the 1982 American Institute of Graphic Arts exhibition of charts, maps, and information graphics used this image of a star designed by Tom Bentkowski. The image reflected Bentkowski's theme for the call for entries to the show: graph paper and three-dimensional letters (A-I-G-A). This idea of wrapping graphs and grids over solid forms perfectly matched the intention of the show, which was to celebrate the new forms of graphic explanation that were appearing with increasing regularity in the press and other media.

56. This art illustrating an article on archeological discoveries of Indian artifacts in large modern-day cities, appeared in the *Boston Globe Sunday Magazine*. The drawing, by Renée Klein, is included here to show how some illustrators use simplified and symbolic images as part of their work. Klein's drawings are full of such direct and lively elements.

51

52

53

54

55

56

Selected Bibliography

Bliss, Charles K. *Semantography-Blissymbolics*. Australia: Semantography-Blissymbolics Publications, 3rd Edition 1978.

Cabarga, Leslie. *A Treasury Of German Trademarks (Volume 1)*. New York: Art Direction Book Company, 1982.

Dreyfuss, Henry. *Symbol Sourcebook*. New York: McGraw-Hill, 1972.

Graphic Design (Magazine). Japan: March, June, September, October, 1971.

Mallery, Garrick. *Picture-Writing Of The American Indians*. New York: Dover Publications, Inc., 1972.

Marples, Morris. *White Horses And Other Hill Figures*. Gloucester, England: Alan Sutton Publishing Ltd., 1949.

Modley, Rudolf. *Handbook Of Pictorial Symbols*. New York: Dover Publications Inc., 1976.

Neurath, Otto. *International Picture Language*. London: Basic English Publishing Company, undated (c. 1937).

Pentagram. *Living By Design*. London: Lund Humphries, 1978.

Stiebner, Erhardt, D. and Urban, Dieter. *Signs + Emblems*. New York: Van Nostrand Reinhold Company Inc., 1984.

Credits

Credits: Except where noted below, all sketches, drawings, and symbols in chapters one to four inclusive are by Nigel Holmes (Chapter two, courtesy *Time* magazine; chapter three, courtesy of Time Inc.) All symbols in chapter five are individually credited in the captions.

Index

Edited by Stephen A. Kliment and Candace Raney
Design by Bob Fillie
Graphic production by Ellen Greene
Test set in 10-point Century Old Style